RICE UNIVERSITY

SEMICENTENNIAL PUBLICATIONS

The People's Architects

EDITOR

HARRY S. RANSOM

THE ARCHITECTS

PIETRO BELLUSCHI

VERNON DeMARS

O'NEIL FORD

CHARLES M. GOODMAN

VICTOR GRUEN

I. M. PEI

JOHN LYON REID

MARSHALL SHAFFER

DRAWINGS BY

CHARLES SCHORRE

The People's Architects

PUBLISHED FOR WILLIAM MARSH RICE UNIVERSITY
BY THE UNIVERSITY OF CHICAGO PRESS

Library of Congress Catalog Card Number: 64-15812

THE UNIVERSITY OF CHICAGO PRESS, CHICAGO & LONDON
The University of Toronto Press, Toronto 5, Canada

Contents

Most of the world's population is gathering in cities. On the salt-water rim of the United States, there will be three giant cities: one extending from Boston to Washington, D.C., another from New Orleans to Houston, and a third from Los Angeles to San Diego. Chicago and Detroit will become one giant fresh-water city. Other great centers of population will develop on the plains. Expansion of this magnitude brings unique problems.

Witness the price of expansion in the last few years across vast areas of the United States. The forests around Boston, New York, Washington, and Chicago have been scraped bare. Life has been drained from the rich swamps around New Orleans. The rolling plains near Tulsa and Omaha have been permanently marred, the spacious beauty destroyed. The beautiful hills around San Francisco have been scarred. Nature's wonders and her calm beauty have been replaced with man-made ugliness. Is this progress, as the developers call it, or is it devastation?

When the population of the world doubles in forty years, will the number of cars double—or triple? The space used to drive and park cars now nearly equals the space taken by homes. Will the number of billboards double? On some roads today the only views available are those contrived by hucksters. Americans apparently want to stack people and cars as high as possible. They don't care where. It can be over a famous landmark such as Grand Central Station or in the middle of a beautiful university campus.

Land is not the only area suffering defacement. The air is being filled with carbon monoxide and evil-smelling gases. The sky is no longer the limit for developers. They pockmark it with enormous crates and even bid for air rights—rights to build above existing buildings. In the future, there may be no view of the sky at all, just as now there is so little view of the landscape.

I

The expanding world of tomorrow will of necessity be a builder's world. It could be a beautiful one. It will not be, if today's wasteful trends continue. Nuclear war is not the only disaster that can befall us. For an equally calamitous scalping of our countryside, let the current, merciless landscrapers continue their wanton destruction of all the natural and potential beauty in our environment.

To stem the current of this man-made devastation, architects must begin to assume leadership in determining the face of tomorrow's world. Hope that this responsibility will be recognized and accepted lies in the existence of a handful of architects who might be dubbed the people's architects. Their interest, expressed through their professional talents, is in the people, and the hope of the people for any beauty in their future world can be placed almost exclusively at these men's feet.

As part of Rice University's semicentennial celebration during the 1962 to 1963 school year, the Department of Architecture honored eight American architects. These are not the only architects doing good work concerned with people. They are representative of the fact that it can be done and that it is hard work. These particular men were singled out because they are a new breed: the hard-nosed pros, who have an innate and highly developed design talent, who possess a deep sensitivity to people's needs, who have a profound feeling of social responsibility, and who have successfully incorporated human values into their buildings. Their goal is to give people houses, schools, churches, hospitals, factories, and shopping centers that are beautiful as well as efficient and economical. Hopefully, there will some day be enough architects such as these to make every market place a stimulating shopping area, to plan dwellings that give inhabitants maximum aesthetic pleasure from their everyday environment, to produce beautiful churches for the inspiration of each worshiper, to plan factories for the stimulus and comfort of workers—as well as the satisfaction of board directors—and to design schools that provide pleasant, efficient surroundings for the growth and development of millions of youngsters.

The individual art and architectural patron has disappeared in America. There are no popes, no kings, no barons with country estates to commission today's buildings. Instead, church committees, developers, city councils, hospital boards, county commissioners, school boards, and the boards of directors of corporations are the commissioning bodies. It is no small task to produce good architecture for committees. It takes great talent and patience to raise the aspirations of a multiheaded client—the building committee. Persuasion, perfection, and great design skill are needed to turn tax money into good architecture. Enormous proficiency is required to produce a beautiful, money-making building for a developer. In spite of these restrictions, some architects have been able to make our influential citizens more architecture-conscious.

This new breed of architects is interested not so much in the expression of personal tastes and favorite forms as in people. These men have a human interest and altruistic sense that sets them apart from other architects. They are people-conscious—and so are their buildings. The architects that Rice University chose to honor belong to no one school of the profession. They live in different regions. They have varying clientele. The scope and character of their projects differ widely. Yet, they have one thing in common—a primary interest in people. This quality is the mark of their greatness.

Harry S Ranson

DIRECTOR OF THE SEMICENTENNIAL
PROGRAM IN ARCHITECTURE

3

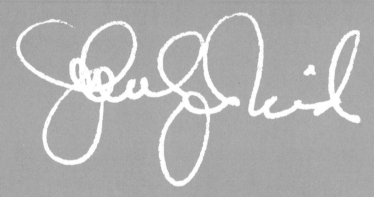

John Lyon Reid's architectural firm in San Francisco is well known for its design of schools; among Mr. Reid's principal works are the Los Cerritos School in South San Francisco (1949); the John Muir School in Martinez, California (1951); and the Lake Merced School in San Francisco (1956). He has been associated with architectural education both at Massachusetts Institute of Technology and at the University of California.

Mr. Reid has extended his work beyond the scope of that of the "average" architect by becoming especially well versed in educational theories and then translating these theories into educational plants. He has based his whole approach to design on the premise that the child is an individual with dignity and importance. According to Mr. Reid, one of the reasons that there exists such a wide disparity between what competent educators believe and what practices are actually followed in education is that school plants generally are geared to traditional, rigidly scheduled programs. He accepts the "growth-development" philosophy, requiring that "groups—small or large—be formed and scheduled at a time, and for a duration, appropriate to the felt needs of the students composing the group." His designs provide spaces for flexible scheduling of students' time and for varying learning experiences, augmenting program requirements to include the creation of an environment conducive to learning.

Mr. Reid has expressed his views in two books, *So You Want To Build a School* and *High Schools—Today and Tomorrow*, as well as in speeches and articles. His designs have received numerous architectural awards.

Rice University has honored John Lyon Reid especially for his design of schools.

We regard achitecture as one of the indicators of civilization and the ability to produce good architecture as one of the skills of a civilized man. Architecture and civilization are inseparable. In addition to the many pleasures that architecture affords to the informed student, it reveals to him an understanding of the people who produced it and the circumstances under which they worked. It is interesting that we can study the architecture of the past, and draw conclusions from it, with a familiarity and assurance that we cannot always summon when we study the architecture we now produce for ourselves.

The term "architecture" is usually understood to apply to a building, but this is unfortunately too narrow a meaning to serve my purposes here. I would prefer to regard "architecture" as meaning the total pattern that man creates on the earth's surface to sustain him, to provide for him, to shelter him, to allow him to travel, and to express what higher aspirations he is moved to express. I think the architect of today may be considered presumptuous when he regards all these as being the "architecture" he has produced, but there is, of course, some historical precedent for his presumption. The Piazza of San Marco in Venice, the plaza in front of St. Peter's together with the whole Vatican complex, the architect Haussmann's plan for Paris, all give some substance for this enlarged view of architecture.

The architect in the most limited definition of his craft is one who concerns himself with the design of a building, large or small. The architect of today is commissioned to design a fraction of the total of the buildings that are constructed, and this is unfortunate, although it is true that he does design the large ones, the public ones, and usually the important ones. The aggregate of all the buildings, whether designed by architects or not, gives form and substance to the environment that is both a setting for and a symbol of our life.

9

The opportunity that exists for the architect to participate in the shaping of our environment when he designs a single building is limited but real; but even then he often finds himself showing a concern for the effect of his building on its neighbors and on its community. In recent years he has more frequently been given the opportunity to plan developments that include more than one building, and this requires the solution to problems of vehicular traffic, utility systems, landscaping and land conservation, and the community uses of land and natural resources. The scope of his work is growing in ever widening circles. He is beginning to look with a professional, although a skeptical, eye on such problems as the design of the entire land and water area of San Francisco Bay and even to such planning problems as the vast regional community extending from Boston to Washington, D.C. When I write of architects in this sense, I mean the whole professional spread of those who participate in the planning of our environment and not only those who are licensed to practice architecture. I suppose the use of the word "architect" in this way is almost as broad as its use when we speak of Winston Churchill as the "architect" of Britain's war strategy.

We have become quite accustomed, with the help of historians, to acquainting ourselves with the people of many historical epochs by examination and study of the architecture they produced. An examination of the architecture we are producing today, no matter whether we take the more limited view of the single building or the enlarged view of the fabric of the region, is not completely reassuring. If we examine critically the larger environmental complex, we are entitled to expect that the same principles of aesthetics might well apply to a region as apply to a building, and that a design incompetence that is regional in scale is no more tolerable than one that occurs in a single building.

But regardless of the scale of the work, our competence to create it, to invest it with some degree of aesthetic content, and our sensitive awareness of this content are measures of how civilized we are.

I have assumed that all of us would agree that most of our urban complexes, when viewed as a whole, are not as well designed as we would wish. It is only recently that any conscious attempt has been made to plan their rehabilitation and growth, and it is too soon to be critical of what architects and planners have been able to accomplish. But so often high property values, traffic habits, and shortsighted business interests have increased the difficulties and reduced the chances of reaching the best solutions. We have had little experience in seeing a community grow over a period of years in accordance with a good plan, and so we find it hard to visualize the amenities that would come out of it. I am afraid that too many Americans accept as inevitable the many disadvantages of the typical city.

It has been one of my professional privileges for almost the last two years to serve the University of California as consulting architect on one of its many campuses, that of the University of California Medical Center in San Francisco. We are starting now on the preparation of a master-plan study for the campus, and one of the participating committees is the Academic Planning Committee, whose responsibility it is to guide the development of the curriculum into the future so that it will serve as one of the bases for the master plan of physical facilities. I have been impressed by the statement of objectives of the medical profession as formulated by this committee. Members of the committee have told me that years ago the medical profession believed its responsibility to be treatment of disease in the individual. Over the years this was changed so that the profession addressed itself to the cultivation of health in the individual. A more recent change holds that the doctor's job is the investigation, treatment, and adjustment of all factors in man's environment so as to sustain man in a state of maximum health. Thus the interest of the medical profession is now enlarged to cover not only its patients' intellectual and physical activity but also their problems of community sanitation, housing, urban noises, smog, traffic, food, and virtually everything that touches the patients' lives. This interest of the profession, which I point out is somewhat an aesthetic one and which is certainly directed toward the larger architectural environment, gives strength to the architect's solicitude about the same thing.

It is my belief that the quality of our architectural output as measured by many standards, of which the aesthetic is of first importance, is not quite as good as our advanced civilization would otherwise lead us to expect, and, unhappily, I believe that only a cultural elite seems to be aware of it. I think that it is appropriate to ask whether or not we are capable of creating a civilized environment for ourselves.

The answer is not to be found alone in the competence of the architect or in the competence of his professional planning and engineering colleagues. The citizenry as a whole, the people the architects and planners work for, participate in the creation of architecture to a degree never before known. I have often wondered whether the architectural greats of a previous generation were able to do their creative thinking and work in artistic isolation, where, like the artist-painter, they had only to answer to their aesthetic and intuitive dictates; perhaps they did not enjoy such enviable freedom. Today the architect has a relatively small amount of freedom of personal artistic decision.

History has not prepared us for the kind of world we find ourselves in today. We know many times more about the world than we ever did before, and we know it with relative suddenness. We probably have not grown in knowledge and wisdom in the balanced and fully rounded sense that the whole man requires. One of the most serious handicaps to the production of a moving, satisfying, and civilized architecture is the lack of common roots, of a tradition, of a shared body of knowledge and culture that unifies and strengthens the people that the architect serves—factors that are necessary if a worthy architecture is to be produced.

Robert Oppenheimer addressed the annual convention of the American Institute of Architects in 1960. He presented some statistics and said hesitantly that these data were not altogether new. They were new to some of us, and to all of us they were disturbing. He told us, for instance, that measured by any quantitative standard at all, such as by the number of people involved, or by the amount of publications appearing, or by the number of patents issued, scientific activity has doubled approximately every ten years during the last two hundred years. Further, he told us that approximately 90 to 93 per cent of all the scientists who had lived and worked in the entire history of civilized man are alive and working today. He said that we knew four times as much about science in 1960 as we did in 1950. Through molecular microbiology, we had gained more insight into the nature of life itself during the preceding five years than had been previously accumulated in the entire history of man. In the field of human behavior, we are moving at a much more sedate pace, since today we only know twice as much as we did twenty years ago.

Such information is disturbing to us because of the terrifying acceleration it reveals in the expansion of our knowledge. The rapidity of this growth is producing such a prodigious total that it is getting farther and farther out of reach of the majority: whether or not we can master this knowledge and use it for our higher purposes is a good question. The gravity of this question does not, however, slow up our pursuit of more knowledge.

I completed my undergraduate work and graduate work at the university level about 1930, and my degrees were evidence of the fact that I had accumulated a few facts and had been able to retain them at least until the appropriate degrees had been conferred. I am sure that these facts I acquired were intended to serve me over a certain period of time, which was never stipulated exactly, nor could it be. In addition to the accumulation of facts, it was assumed that I had an attitude of inquiry and an interest in acquiring more knowledge—and a respect for it. All this would help form my attitude toward life, its problems and opportunities. I assume, too, that those who decided in their wisdom that I had earned a degree felt that in some way I showed the beginning of a development of my own philosophy, an awareness of the problems and travails of myself and my fellow man, a hope and an eagerness on my part that I might contribute to their solution, and a belief in the importance of that contribution, no matter how meager. Some of those facts that I had accumulated decreased in importance or lost their validity much sooner than I had anticipated and, I am sure, sooner than anticipated by my universities. A man may now expect that he will be required to renew himself four times in his lifetime if he to keep his stock of facts current.

This represents one of the major problems of those who engage in a life of intellectual activity, and I suspect that there are more people today than ever before who live, work, and produce through activities that are substantially intellectual. The so-called three learned professions, law, medicine, and theology, have not for a long time defined the limits of the intellectual life.

The productive potential of the machine has for some years been affecting our lives and making its changes in our ways of living. Lewis Mumford believes that one of our major problems stems from our inability to master the machine. Be that as it may, the machine has not only assisted us in the search for knowledge but now drives us to seek more. The time that it has given us has freed a greater percentage of people than ever before to search and inquire.

More knowledge and the limits of the human mental capacity lead us, whether we like it or not, to specialization. For most of my own life I have been superficially familiar, at least, with the problems of the medical specialist. My brother-in-law is a surgeon, and I have been conversationally exposed to his problems for thirty years; recently my work with the University of California Medical Center has permitted me to listen to discussions of the problems of educating the doctor. We hear of the specialties of the eye, the blood, the allergy, the virus, the brain, and the gland. It is recognized that the treatment of the whole man and his health cannot be handled by an accumulation of specialists; and this has led to the emergence of another specialist, the diagnostician. This situation has a direct effect on the cost of achieving and maintaining health, and the doctor is fully aware of the dilemma he and we face. The elimination of the specialist is not necessarily the answer, particularly if we are to pursue the complex and related chains of knowledge that are accumulating. The age of the specialist is not about to end but, if anything, to intensify.

And that presents one of the major dilemmas of contemporary life. Our knowledge, it seems, is being developed by those who have only indirect communication, if any at all, with the man upon whose life their knowledge has such an impact. This is true in an age where the technique of communication has reached a high level of development. Man has traveled around this world in ninety minutes, and we are now talking about a commercial transportation service to carry a man from New York to San Francisco in about one and one-half hours. The present figure of four and one-half hours was a dream a few years ago. We can now transmit live television pictures from Europe to America. I have talked with ease on the telephone between Algiers and San Francisco. The problems of one hundred and fifty million people are now the problems of two and one-half billion.

While the physical instruments of communication are being constantly developed and improved, there seems to be a gap in intellectual communication that is not bridged. That gap is measured in terms of the limits of individual capacity and our mounting fund of knowledge. One man can't know everything there is to know, and we cannot help him by stopping the search. Not only will his curiosity urge him, but the scientific tradition will encourage him, to penetrate deeper and deeper into the field of his interest. The continuing quest for knowledge offers a trap of esoteric specialization which is difficult to avoid as our knowledge deepens. The more we find out through specialized research, the more we become aware of the bonds which interrelate all knowledge. The dissolving of the barriers between the fields of knowledge does not simplify the problems which our high degree of specialization creates for us.

The term "Renaissance man" probably did not originate during the Renaissance but rather appeared much later as we began to sense our own inability to synthesize our stockpile of facts into a philosophy that had meaning and pertinence for us. Leonardo da Vinci is the name that first comes to mind when we think of the "Renaissance man." He was no doubt possessed of incredible intellectual powers and must be recognized by everyone as one of the great artists in our Western tradition. He was a sculptor, a painter, an architect; he was a naturalist, a geologist, a chemist, a mathematician, and an astronomer; he was a maker of musical instruments and a musician; he engaged in metalwork, he made jewelry, he studied anatomy, and he was a designer of pageants. He was a writer and a poet. There is some evidence that he knew something about weaving and that in his younger days he was a strong man and an athlete of sorts. He was an expert in the arts and weapons of war. Because of his work and studies the aircraft of today would not be an unexpected sight for him.

Even with his knowledge of scientific matters, he probably would be regarded today as a dilettante and a dabbler. I doubt if even his powers of intellect would permit him to penetrate as deeply today into as many fields of knowledge as they did in his day. It did not require an intellect of Leonardo's stature to acquire a sufficient mastery of the knowledge of the times to synthesize it into a philosophy that was necessary to act with skill, grace, and even intellectual reward in the life of the day. With the evidence we now have of the breadth and depth of Renaissance civilization, I would assume that an elite, of some numbers, existed that possessed a meaningful philosophy of life and some mastery of man's range of knowledge. Today this is infinitely more difficult, if not impossible, for even a smaller elite.

It appears to me, then, that today we have an unfortunately narrow band over which we can communicate. The scientist or the engineer, whose work may have a great impact on the life, the habits, and the thinking of all of us, can with difficulty, if at all, interpret his work to the man in the street. That this is so seldom done must not be overlooked as one of the causes of the tensions and maladjustments of the contemporary scene. At those times in the history of civilization when man has felt that he was capable of leading a civilized life and was leading it, there was a capacity for communication and an understanding that was broad, at least in terms of the dimension of man's knowledge at the time. The peak of Renaissance civilization as we know it showed a constructive and creative activity in the political life, in which people not only participated actively, and I presume with intelligence, but sustained an interest in their government and themselves. These and the affairs of the market place and world of the arts are all a part of a life of intellectual vigor and challenge requiring a comprehensive insight into the structure of the whole society by its citizens.

If the extent and complexity of our knowledge have created serious problems, their positive contributions are so obvious and so significant that they should not be diminished by a one-sided view of the whole matter. Poverty, want, and hunger have come closer to the vanishing point than at any time in history. In their place we have achieved an abundance that is a problem in itself and a standard of comfort, choice, and service in our day-to-day life; we hope the prospect of continually increasing leisure will not be a problem. All these, if we are able to shape them into the structure we want for society, hold tempting prospects.

One of the most serious problems of the architect today is the meagerness of the bond of common interest, of common roots and traditions and of the area of popular commune. The architect, with his eye on the civilization he is helping to shape, is too often unhappy and dissatisfied with the results of his professional efforts and seeks reasons for it. Although there are many distinguished buildings in the United States which have been built in recent years, the percentage seems to him to be too low. The architect does not like the environment, both urban and suburban, that is emerging; he wishes that more people would be constructively dissatisfied with it. Architecture and the total environment of which it is a part are measures of our intellectual stature and symbols of our artistic maturity or immaturity. The architect hopes that between him and his fellow citizens, the non-architects, there would exist a common interest, a tradition, an avenue of communication, that would enable them jointly to create a more fitting total environment. If the quality of architecture today is something less than we deserve, it is regrettable. If it is a barometer of intellectual and artistic maladjustment, it is even more regrettable.

The architect today does not have the strength, the independence, the authority, or for that matter, the wisdom to design a civilized environment singlehanded; the structure of society instead delineates relationships which virtually require action by groups to do the job. The difficulty the architect faces is the result of a conflict between two apparently irreconcilable factors: first, that the significance architecture has for us is as a work of art and that as such it is the creation of an individual; and second, that the temper of the times inclines us, even forces us, to group action. Our reverence for the democratic process does not dispose us to confer on the artist the right to make artistic decisions, especially when they are personal ones, and especially when they shape a public architecture. Whether or not democracy can be made to understand the artistic process is a moot question. The more culturally enlightened the members of a democratic society become, the greater, I am sure, will be the understanding of the artistic process and the greater the willingness to let the artist be an artist.

For the present, at least, architecture is produced by a rather remarkable process of group action. Let me describe for you a few of the specifics of this group effort as I have seen it and some of the problems that the architect and the citizen face, as together they give form to our environment. In my own professional work I have had the opportunity to design a great many public school buildings, for which the client has been the public, represented by the school board. This board is composed of a cross section of the community, and members come from the professions, from business, and from the home. A school building in some ways is a mirror that reflects with the least distortion the expression of community desires and intent. For me, school buildings and churches are unusual and special challenges to the architect in that the design can be resolved only in part on grounds of function, cost, and time schedule. These three things invariably arise as criteria for school buildings, since they are easy to understand and to handle in a public discussion; and, too, I do not deny their importance. But there are design overtones, especially in these two types of projects, which are for the architect the nature and the essence of the problem and of the challenge. Without being at all sentimental about it, the architect likes to think when he is designing a school building that he is offering a sound and businesslike answer to matters of function, cost, and time schedule and also that he is planting in a community a symbol of education expressed in concrete and steel which shows the importance of education and which stands in some mystical way as an emblem of faith in children and hope for their future. And, of course, these latter criteria are ultimately the only measures of value.

I suppose that it is quite unrealistic of me to say that altogether too few public communities have recognized this challenge that so many of my architect colleagues have seen in the design of school buildings; too few value a completed school building for those things that make it an inspired answer to this challenge. Most school buildings in America that have been built in the last fifteen years are adequate and certainly better as educational instruments than those that were being built in 1900; some of them are distinguished, and a very few of them are inspired. I would like to raise the percentage. To improve our schools now requires only two things: a desire to improve them and a common agreement on what an inspired school building might be. The first, the desire, is not the subject of this paper; but the second is—the breadth of knowledge, a common understanding, a tradition that would unite an architect and a public for creative accomplishment. This is not often found and, I repeat, is the greatest deterrent to a distinguished architecture that I know today.

Recently the federal government authorized a nation-wide competition to select a design and an architect for a memorial to Franklin Delano Roosevelt to be located in Washington, D.C. When the results of the judgment of the competition were announced, there were heated debates regarding the winning designs, and these debates occurred not only within the profession but with equal enthusiasm and heat in the press and among the public in general. At the present time, I believe, congressional hearings regarding the competition, the judgment, and the winning designs are still in progress. It is my opinion that there will not be sufficient agreement among all of the lay and professional people involved to permit the project to be built. In fact, I am not at all hopeful that in the present public and professional climate a monument of this importance could ever be built.

The public shows itself in many different ways as it exerts its influence on architecture. In the public-school building and in the Roosevelt competition, the participation and the voice of the public is firsthand and direct. It may show itself in a much more indirect way where state rules, regulations, and administrative procedures embody habits, attitudes, and, in some cases, obscured objectives. The public influence on architecture may show itself in ways that are usually perceived by architects and by few others because of the purely professional and specialized nature of the involvement; the public, not being involved as a first party, is seldom aware of the strength of its influence on design. For instance, the urban environment, particularly in that part of it that is built by private capital, is shaped by a myriad of influences which are not strictly architectural and which in this sense are public, for example, tax laws, considerations of property value, zoning laws, building codes, legal controls, and advertising necessities that are overwhelming and bewildering to the lay person and little short of it for the architect. Out of this man-made complexity, we probably could not at the present time create a civilized environment, even if we wanted to. This complexity of laws and regulations and the lack of common goals and enlightened standards must carry a large responsibility for today's architecture. Too seldom will a public client be strongly moved by common goals and too often will chances for success go down the drain in the conflicts and compromises of group action. Any project that successfully survives all this faces further hazards at the state level. The state of California has produced a formidable body of rules and regulations which govern the design and construction of public school buildings and which may require during the course of a project one hundred and forty-seven approvals of public agencies before the completion of construction. We are more fortunate in Texas, where only about six are required.

The architect often finds himself working on large and important commissions with a corporate body of one kind or another as the client. It is interesting that some of the corporate enterprises of America show sophistication and enlightenment and that they build distinguished buildings in both urban and suburban settings that set high standards for their communities. This is quite obviously not due alone to the quality of architectural service they employ, since one corporate body will often employ several architects, each working separately on different projects, with over-all good results. This has happened with enough frequency that one wonders whether or not a small group of well-educated men (could I call it a "cultural elite"?) in the corporate management was responsible for the results.

Today the architect does his work most often in varied kinds of collaborative efforts with varied public bodies. Less frequently does he work with the individual client. There are notable exceptions, however. I knew an individual with an intense interest in creative design who occupied a position of authority in a corporate structure and who found himself able to provide a leadership that attracted and encouraged the finest kind of creative artist: Walter Paepke of the Container Corporation of America was such a person. But most often the forces that are so important today in their effect on artistic expression, on architecture, and on our environment as a whole are those that arise from the activities and policies of the organization rather than the discriminating individual.

Automobiles today owe their appearance to stylists—specialists who carry out the findings of a public opinion poll, which is interpreted to them by the public relations department; I suppose that this shows that the public has now taken over the design of automobiles and has superseded the automobile designer-craftsman. The architect so far has been able to show a little more strength in his tussle against public taste.

To recapitulate for a moment a few of the things we have talked about: (*a*) For many reasons which are unique to the times in which we now live, we find it increasingly hard to share interests, to understand each other, and to communicate. We are separated, not enriched, by our differences. (*b*) If we look for it, we can quite easily see this in our architecture, because (*c*) the artistic, intuitive, and personal choices of the individual architect which are necessary to a distinguished architecture are becoming less important in the creation of today's architecture than the influences, both direct and indirect, which arise through public participation. (*d*) If I am right in thinking that a distinguished architecture is desirable and that it can be achieved, if I am right in attaching great importance to the public influence and participation in the creation of our contemporary architecture, if I am right in thinking that we will not find our best in architectural design until our common bonds are strengthened and deepened—then what next?

It is of little consequence to question which is more important, the architecture which has failed as yet to reach its potential high-water mark or the cultural inadequacy it reveals. I am sure that there is little disagreement that both are important and that the climate in which architecture reaches its full flower will similarly nourish our cultural growth. Among the many strengths of our society, public education is probably the greatest. It probably involves more individuals than any other single effort we make. The operations of the national educational effort are not reserved for an elite segment of our people but rather touch in varying degrees almost everyone. The effectiveness and the methods of our educational system have received and are receiving a great deal of attention and criticism. I cannot help but point out, parenthetically, that much of it is unfavorable and much of it is uninformed and unfair. We are quick to blame our educators for our inability to match immediately every Soviet accomplishment, for the alleged physical unfitness of our armed forces, for juvenile delinquency, and for the national crime rate, and I suppose it would be consistent to hold our educators responsible for what I believe to be a noticeably small bond of common intellectual ground that holds our nation and perhaps our civilization together. It is my belief, and one that I hold with conviction, that public education is far less responsible for this than are we as a whole, that educators are aware of this problem and have been attempting to cope with it with what I believe to be encouraging success. If this success is more limited than we would wish, it can be attributed rather to the national temper than to the ineffectiveness of education. This is a problem, however, that I think can only be solved by education, and it must be dealt with at all levels of education, not in the universities alone.

When I was on the faculty of the Massachusetts Institute of Technology, I remember the deep concern that was felt about the responsibility of the Institute to educate the whole man, and I remember the decision to form a School of Humanities to broaden the educational experience of the students in what then seemed to me a most unlikely place, an institution devoted so completely to science and engineering. So many institutions at the university level offering specialized and professional training now give increasing emphasis to the humanities. I see the greatest hope for the solution of the problems I have attempted to describe in attaching even more importance than we do now to studies in this field. The scope of our knowledge today is vast indeed. How do we assimilate it, understand it, and make it serve us?

In relatively recent years man has shown a spectacular skill in the fields of science and engineering which has yielded the even more spectacular accomplishments which are the symbols of our time. If we are less skilled and less accomplished in the arts, I think it can be linked to the weakness of the cultural bond that holds us together. It seems to me that the great task which faces education today, and particularly at the university level, is a twofold one: to encourage and to implement the pursuit of knowledge no matter how deep or esoteric the penetration into the unknown; and to broaden and elevate the level of human discourse, to strengthen our roots and the traditions common to all of us, to extend to the widest conceivable dimension the band over which the intellectual, artistic, and humanitarian interests of all people extend. The second, in particular, presents to the universities a task and a challenge of greatest importance.

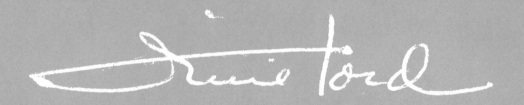

O'Neil Ford centers his practice of architecture in San Antonio, Texas, but his projects extend throughout the United States and abroad.

Mr. Ford's background is as varied as his practice. His formal education was in English and physics. Through extensive reading and actual experience, he became trained in architectural design. He is especially well acquainted with the indigenous pioneer architecture of Texas and Louisiana and has also studied antecedents such as early Christian architecture and English Georgian work. He has done etching and lithographing and has made furniture and lighting fixtures. Materials and their use are important to him: he has searched for more beautiful materials not commonly available on the market; he has encouraged local manufacturers to improve their products. He has done a great deal of research and experimentation involving structural systems as resources for architectural design, in particular the applications of lift-slab, prestressed concrete, and shell construction. He feels that it is through the marriage of many elements—site planning, construction and methods of building, sensitive use of materials, the contributions of related arts—that a distinctive architectural expression emerges. For him, architecture is "the art of building spaces which are to be used—and doing it tastefully, decently, and with a strong idea."

Mr. Ford has been honored by Rice University especially for his design of industrial buildings.

I read much history, many technical articles, all possible literature about materials, systems, and devices, but I cannot bring myself to read the voluminous spewing of philosophy and esoteric writing that architects, editors, and critics are producing today. The adulation, deification, and omniscient postures of most architectural magazine writers seem to say little that is related to the man, the lines, the specifications, and the judgment—yes, judgment and discernment —that make good buildings. Nevertheless, my reaction to literary and conversational architecture is not so far from the center as my son's definition of architecture—"the stuff that is piled against the force of gravity and wind, and then leaks, cracks, and finally falls down." He may be as right as the glorifiers.

I am an avid listener, however, when sincerity and enthusiasm characterize an individual, a writer, or a group's search for answers. When a student, or hopefully, an alive young architect, gathers to discuss architecture with his betters, his equals, or his professors, he finds causes, reasons, enthusiasm, moments of disgust, and some boasting expressed with refreshing earnestness. He answers, agrees, or stands his ground until the exchange is interrupted and the group is ejected by the bored proprietor. The talk continues under the lamps, and though nothing is resolved, the interchange is a creative exercise unhampered by time, economics, or any pragmatic demand. Recently, in Paris, I listened to such a colloquy that didn't gain momentum until midnight or resolve itself by dawn. As I drank the last of many strong coffees, I wondered how the adult architect—the hard-pressed practitioner—could ever find a similar stimulus in a group of his confreres, at a convention or in any of the journals that arrive on his desk every month. That experience in Paris was barely different from one in London where the students from the A.A. (Architectural Association School of Architecture) generated a violent roar, a fierce fight over the way things are taught in architectural schools, the way buildings are planned and built, and the way things are written about the way things are built. Watching these fine performances and proudly hearing the discourses of several American students in the groups, I was pleased to listen. I wondered when I had been to an A.I.A. meeting, a convention, or a public lecture where any strong or even weak sentiments were so fervently expressed about architecture. I have watched all of us become ethical professionals who scrupulously avoid and evade every subject or situation that might slightly imply our incompetence or the infrequence of any superior accomplishments.

A heavy cloud covers my thoughts as I ponder the gap between the freshness and idealism of these unusual students and the trivial and vulgar works of builders, architects, and developers that eventually appear and make up the negative nothingness of our streets and their positive ugliness. It is not just that contented egoism and adamant huckstering have made our country so irreparably ugly but that all the brackets of privileges and restraints that our great founders put on paper and so seriously and profoundly pledged seem so brutally abridged or selfishly interpreted by the "go-getters" and "not doers." These good founding precepts were not abstract prognostications but were the sharp, clear, and sensitively framed structure for the projection of an imaginative idea and a sensible civilization. The means and methods were clearly stated.

All physical ugliness and social ugliness have strong concomitants and roots. Incredibly, there is rampant today all manner of hate and fierce argument on the basic idea—of all things—of civil rights. Today our great privileges are so flaunted and license so condoned that in some of our cities 30 per cent of the citizens live in slums. Not just the physical man is crushed, but all rights, equalities, opportunities, and self-respect go down. It seems, therefore, not a crooked analogy to lock hand-in-hand the bitter disregard for the rights of others with the callous notion that a man may put up anything ugly, vulgar, or trivial he wishes so long as it is "big enough" and he has the money. Can you think how seriously tragic it is that any congressman or lawmaker, anywhere, can find a reason or the audacity to speak against the civil rights of any man or group of men? Isn't it indeed strange that in this land of billboards, ugly poles and wires, pop architecture and slums, we have as a complementary and parallel circumstance the monstrous idea that if a Samaritan loves his fellow man, fights for another's causes, simply does something for him, then he is a "bleeding heart"? Is it not incredible that if a man has intellectual attainments, or even intellectual curiosity, he may be labeled an egghead—this, in a country frantic to advance every curriculum to excellence, from the first grade to graduate study? Is the student who carries a stack of good phonograph records under his arm really a "longhair" or an "odd"? Is the young man who wears a beret more effeminate than the one who wears a Homburg? It is evident that the student or any man who cares more deeply about what he does than what he receives for it, architect included, must expect pointing fingers. An attack on personal rights, pursuits, and nonconformity of all kinds does seem like an attack on gravity, growth, and life itself.

This physical and social ugliness is producing a very real and shocking effect on the youth of our country. The usurpation and defamation of land by vulgarians and the construction of square miles of shacks have given us a generation of children with blinders built on both sides of their heads and minds. They move along our city streets, looking through a narrow slit, seeing nothing as they pass, and seeking only the decent places they know—their houses, their school rooms, their green playgrounds—where there is release and relief from the billboards, the dull architecture, and the flamboyant huckstering. Like sightless fish in deep ocean holes, they know not what they see or what they do not see. They have few discriminative powers; their standards *are* the billboards, the insistent neon signs, the black poles, transformers, and wires, the ugly lettering, the "misleading" advertising, the Perma-Stone houses. The wrong things men build cry out "impulse selling and buying." Last week, one of my children saw the point for a moment. As we drove along in our mental and visual parenthesis, we noticed a sign which read "Beware of Imitations—This Is a Genuine Perma-Stone Installation." We laughed, but not enough to shake the horrible house. So, we, and to a greater degree, our children, become unobservant as this ugliness creeps like a prairie fire, as towns lose their edges, as the separation of towns becomes more and more blurred by junk, by incomprehensible expressway intersections, by a system of speed roads that completely ties the man to strict observance and sharpened skill in a race through ugliness to his hut or to his castle.

In our marvelously engineered 300 horsepower steeds, in our bigger and longer compacts with appropriate chrome, stamped ridges, and bulges, we look over the extensive deck shining ahead of us, and without stretching our necks or moving ourselves at all, we see wonders of motels and restaurants and other sights of South Main in Houston. After we pass the big exclamation point, "The Shamrock," South Main becomes as noisy, brash, and vulgar as close-in Main Street was dull and decaying. As we progress northward on Preston Road in Dallas, the blaze of "selling pieces" is only momentarily interrupted by the chic of the Neiman-Marcus Store. A longer, more strident commercial effort vies for one's attention as one moves through the varied splendor of Colfax in Denver. Who has seen the sad things that Tucson and Phoenix have become? Have you seen the road to Alamogordo as it stretches through El Paso's own special neon slum? Who knows Ayres Street in Corpus Christi? Driving from the great prairies toward the corporate limits, the first establishments to greet the visitor are vast wrecked-car lots—acres of them, and growing. Then, through a fantastic variety of nasty architecture and nasty signboards, one makes his treeless way toward the bay, and not until he has reached the bluff is there any relief from the mess—the incredibly mediocre buildings. There is not time to recount the hideous accomplishments in Los Angeles, and we know they will become more numerous, but the city's sad influence on the surrounding desert towns is sickening. One expects little from Los Angeles, Reno, and Las Vegas, the latter two particularly having neither purpose nor direction, but it is jolting to see the environs of Palm Springs, Palm Desert, El Indio, and a sad string of sloppy towns all the way to El Paso. This condition has spread where one scarcely expects it. The same disfigurement grows apace in Nashville and Charlotte, and the frilly grille-work of New Orleans seems a little silly in competition with the real gillifrass of the fringes. Finally, there is Oklahoma City! Its highways, leading from town into the Oklahoma prairie, may well exhibit the most miserable clutter of them all.

On the other end of the scale is the equally depressing variety and over-effort of Idlewild Airport, through which I have passed innumerable times. There are a few reasonably pleasant spots on the grounds, but there is almost no place for the traveler. Furthermore, he feels scaled to midget size while he is being pushed through the bewildering pattern of the dismal Big Plan of the place.

Do we condone this; do we really fight it? Do the Australians and people of Toronto know that they, too, are being swallowed by this appalling and ever accelerating growth? Are we, as architects and planners, entirely impotent in the face of this irresponsible triumph of the vulgarians? How do we answer when we are confronted by a list of monstrous structures in Houston and discover that many of the buildings and the exotic signs were designed by architects. Many of the multicolored motels, capital EAT places, and capital BEER places came from the offices of honorable and upstanding citizen architects. They have chosen not to put themselves above the hucksters, or below them, but shoulder to shoulder. For example, there are the sure-footed, supermarket designers who are quick to adopt any cliché, trick, or showy device that they see published in a magazine or that wins some institutional award, for they are set and ready for solid adoption or enlargement. I should not speak of the spread of Sheep Dog screens that are used across the fronts of so many buildings. I have never done one, and it seems that I am always late to see the value of such wildly accepted innovations. We are busy building just buildings, so we haven't time for serious thought about screens, glass blocks, corner windows, great sign pylons over rock and cactus entrance gates until they are widely recognized as old-hat. Every now and then one sees the ingenious perforated screens that seem to be the main purpose for building at all. They are, I believe, quite as solid a general panacea as Perma-Stone is at a lower level.

Just a month ago I heard an architect and engineer heatedly debate whether a concrete block wall costing $.80 a square foot would support a gorgeous concrete curtain costing $6.00 a square foot. I observed that the windows, vents, and walls were placed in disorder, befitting the disorderly plan, and that the shaggy screen would do wonders for this disorder of openings that were scattered vertically, horizontally, and differently on all façades. It seems proper, we observe, that Corbusier never seemed to worry about his disorder in the openings at Ronchamp as they pushed inward and outward. He knew precisely where he wanted them. It is refreshing to know that Corbusier's copycats soon find themselves on a dead limb. As soon as the derivers sense the freedom of his "disorder," they pounce upon it and vigorously apply it. The great man's sudden abandonment of a system or device must be bewildering. The copyists must come to quick stops and begin their adulation and rationalization all over again, as the master moves in his own creative sphere— rightly or wrongly, beautifully or sometimes clumsily.

All the boards in architectural schools now carry the burden of weighty and shaggy concrete blobs, and this, mixed with the Lincoln Log concrete style so affectionately fostered in several schools, may well produce a coarseness close to that period following the Columbian Exposition. What the early 1900's did to the classic orders will be and is being done to Ronchamp.

Just a few years ago the fad in hundreds of schools was the stiff and stringy drawings of the Followers of Mies. It was a hard and sharp contest with thin lines and sheer stretches of invisible walls—or no walls. They understood neither the weaknesses nor the strengths of Mies. Between these tiresome and extended rituals came thin shells. All the students, all the professors, all the competitors, set them side by side by the thousands. This fashion in models and string flourished while Mr. Candela continued to build his inexpensive warehouses and factories in which he employed the blossom and tent shapes to cover big spaces with good design and interesting shapes, using cheap labor and materials. Soon the highways sported motels and filling stations with entrance features that were shells or nearly shells, and the superficial resemblance covered the timbers, wires, metal lath, and stucco. So quickly did the hucksters sieze on the possibilities of this new and more exotic form that conscientious architects and enthusiastic students were forced to declare this feature passé even before they had learned the structural principles involved. The real inherent advantages of the hyperbolic paraboloid were never fully understood.

I believe our office and our associates may very well have designed more buildings using these beautiful shells than any other in the country. We used it as a good principle should be used, aesthetically and structurally, as a beautiful and cheap way to make a big span-cover of concrete. We devised forms and erection systems that fitted the economics and techniques of the United States, and we tested and tested until we felt that we understood the limitations and the possibilities. Sometimes they stood for everyone to see; sometimes they did their job behind solid walls; but always they served a special purpose—structurally, aesthetically, and economically. It did not occur to us to give a name to this system any more than we felt the need to write poems for bar joists, wood studs, laminated beams, lamella frames, or post and beam and deck systems. Years ago, when our office shared in the research and pioneering of the lift-slab system, we were amazed at the glossy stories and papers written about this obviously sensible way to build the conventional flat concrete floor or roof. We began by assuming that it would be faster and cheaper to lift all the ingredients at one time in one piece. Within the proper limits of span and height, this idea is quite as good today as it was on its "discovery" day in 1948. It is a carefully researched and gradually developed system of lifting. The objects lifted may be concrete slabs, grillage of beams, bridges, or concrete and steel space frames. This system has also been used to raise great domes and long trusses. It is simpler to pour concrete and place steel on the ground, simpler to fabricate trusses or frames at normal walking level, and simpler and quicker to lift them completely assembled and in one piece with machines. Just the other day I was asked, "Do you still jack up the old slabs?" Another person asked if I was still on the old shell jag? I could have answered "Yes, and I am still on the brick kick and the column and beam kick, and I shamelessly make big glass walls now and then." So goes the frittering and the quick abandonment of basic systems, basic ideas, useful developments—our "vocabulary" and our tools.

Who remembers the blare of triumph when curtain walls were discovered just a few years ago? There were many round table discussions and workshop studies about these new walls. The magazines piled up pages of praise and appraisal on the subject. Now "curtain walls" is a nasty phrase—perhaps it always was a little silly—but this doesn't alter the fact that the prefabricated wooden walls of Gloucester are beautiful, that La Coruña in northern Spain shows whole streets of splendid squares of wood frames and glass, that Switzerland has whole fronts set up in one fine frame of wood panels and window panels. On a back street near New York's City Hall is a Singer Building with beautifully constructed façades of iron frames and terra-cotta panels built long before the more recent and famous Singer Building. In their places, these early structures represented a builder's way of building and not another seller's fashion.

Just recently, the arch has been discovered. The bright Chicago architect Harry Weese has designed a brick schoolhouse with Fall-River-Line-Factory style segmented windows. Now, students who had believed that architecture began with the Lovell house are giving hours to discussion of this new frankness. The arch will soon be given much printed space, and it will be defended in strong philosophical terms as a fine, sound, new thing and a shaping force. Supporting evidence to this effect will be profusely provided. Examples will be shown of Carmel and San Jose missions, the Liverpool docks, and Richardson's big stone arches. Brunelleschi and Michelozzo will be given space and humble credit. Most important will be the gushy praise for the men or preferably the man who showed the courage, etc., etc. Precisely so have some architects discovered the Doge's Palace and Lincoln Logs.

When will some teacher in some school learn that he must teach the whole of architecture as it has grown, bloomed, and decayed, the results having been sometimes humble and beautiful, sometimes pompous and beautiful, sometimes brilliantly and even laboriously devised, or sometimes—in the indigenous vernacular—just grown? When will the extraordinary pleasure of learning about architecture be made more significant by presenting the subject not just in dull, contrived, academic chronology but in solid, analogous parallel to all history? There must be a way to discern the significance of all process and change instead of memorizing only the bold incidents and typical monuments.

On the occasion of the announcement of his retirement as dean at the University of California, William Wilson Wurster said:

Architecture is a corridor with many doors, opening into all aspects of human life. It unites many, many forces. I do not believe in embalming ideas. We, none of us, architects or others, have the privilege of building monuments to ourselves. Our work must be for people. I don't pretend to be a great teacher. I was a good administrator running fences for good teachers—my forte is in making it possible for things to happen. I do not teach facts, but teach as a process of arriving at facts. . . .

It seems to me that this uncalculated statement is a well-rounded premise for good thinking and good architecture. The works of Mr. Wurster's office are wonderfully unalloyed and artlessly direct. Their influence has been good and lasting. I have heard the great Finn, Aalto, make a similar statement, and I have seen his factories, mills, and schools standing so forthright, so useful, so very beautiful. They were done with spirit and passion. The need for philosophy did not go into their making nor is there a need for subtle explanations or clever labels for the finished product.

Is it not true that architecture is the enclosing of useful and beautiful space with sound and beautiful covering? It does not lessen the art that architecture has economic and structural limitations that prevent its being an abstraction in process or in the work itself. It seems right, however, to assume that these limitations should eliminate the arbitrariness of philosophical guessing and prognostication that is so prevalent today.

I have had occasion to see the work in many schools of architecture during the past twenty years. I feel that during ten years of this period these schools produced a kind of directionless wallowing between real creativity and the idolatrous rigidity of imitation of Mies, Wright, Gropius, Nervi, Candela, and others. Recently, at least three important schools have narrowed their casting to expert imitation—in words and in drawings—of the well-known precepts and works of their respective deans or directors. I do not presume to make judgment of the wearing quality of the works and words of the head men at Harvard, Yale, or the University of Pennsylvania, but I am well aware of the incredible inflexibility of the recent graduates who have studied at these and other schools where strong men reign. The formula is strongly circumscribed, and the explanation and rationalization is sophisticated and full of special phraseology. The men who emerge from these schools are well-finished products in a rather narrow area and attitude. I believe very few of Mr. Kahn's students understand that in his rich language, broad awareness, and personal capacity great things dwell. Instead, these students spread across the land with pat notions, a package of details, and a whole stock of thin analogies. Worse yet, they somehow manage to acquire the veil of cynicism that comes with the worship of a master. I can't imagine Mr. Kahn's wanting this.

Recently, I arrived at one of these citadels and observed the preliminaries to a jury session. When a half-dozen models, carried in by bleary-eyed students, were set in a row before the wise elders, I was astonished to see that they were as alike and as faithful to the dogma as the 1963 Chevrolets, Pontiacs, Fords, and Chryslers. The variations were superficial and arbitrary, and scale was uniformly disregarded. These products of weeks of deliberation, cutting, and gluing were devoid of any strong individuality. There was no indication that they were related to any material beyond cardboard and plastic. All were equally unfinished; all were essentially the same thing. The hair-splitting declamations and exclamations were tiresome and almost repetitive; the language was abstruse and the manner almost diffident. This is the essence of the brand of cynicism that pervades a lot of teaching and learning today.

Somehow the architect and the student of architecture have missed the pleasures of curiosity, study, and search for the meaning and significance of all building that has ever been done. The strong tendency to set patterns, programs, and overprecise prescriptions in the curriculum has resulted in a series of prolonged, but eventually abandoned, dogmas. The young man who is finally licensed between the ages of thirty and thirty-two has forgotten most of the mathematics and chemistry he didn't need in the first place. He has listened to the fancy language, has known the twenty or thirty men who teach, but has come out a well-squared expert in an overdeveloped, over-personal religion of style with sharp boundaries.

I have talked and worked with men who have come from the several "important" schools, and after a short time their work and their attitudes were no different, no better, no worse, on the whole than the same characteristics and accomplishments of men from schools less well known. I am repeatedly surprised that quite often the good but not outstanding schools produce men who have more curiosity about history, about the immediate environment, about the special indigenous character of local buildings and materials.

I have heard several of the big architects say that architecture is a business. No one can deny that busy offices must give certain attention to money and deadlines, but I believe the whole consideration of architecture as a "business," big or little, is wrong. The hundred biggest offices in this country seem to produce much undistinguished architecture. Worse yet is the architect who really believes that the most important thing is to "get the job." I cannot fully express my disgust with this attitude. Recently, I read only the title of an article by the editor of a "Home" or "Merchant Homes" magazine which stated, "Now in 1963—Selling IS MORE IMPORTANT THAN BUILDING!!"

For architects, all the education, research, study, design, analysis, drafting, specifying, and inspecting serves one purpose; that, of course, is building. I am often a little alarmed that our estimable and useful architectural society, the American Institute of Architects, puts too much emphasis on public relations. The temptation seems to be to follow the advertisers who oversimplify the process of creating and overemphasize the desirability of the product.

What architect would want himself leveled to professional-society average so that he and all the others of better or worse qualifications could be packaged and sold to the public? I want no cellophane wrapper on a slick "how to hire an architect" kit or "how to hook a client" kit that fits me or anyone into a neat slot of conformity. I read our *Journal,* which is now certainly one of the best publications architects have ever had, and I am grateful for provocative articles, for good critical essays, for purely pragmatic information, for its attention to history and conservation; but now and then the huckstering creeps in.

I am amused that almost every regional convention of the A.I.A. makes adequate provision for a golf tournament; I am more amused when I see architect friends who are most anxious to display their skill on the fairway, as if it were a real tool of the trade. I went to one convention where there was, so help me, a bridge tournament on the program! At the same convention, much time was spent with a slick salesman who had been engaged, or was hoping to be hired, to write a series of booklets and brochures on "What the Architect Is and Does." The joke is that this would not be a description of what the best architects do but a recital of the procedure, fees, etc., common to all members.

We are at present planning a house for a Houston woman—a good, simple wooden house with no tricks and, so far, no excuses. I would be absolutely embarrassed to hand her a neat little booklet about our fees, our virtues, and the standards of nobility of *all* architects. She knows what an architect is, surely suspects the weaknesses, appreciates the effort toward excellence—the effort to solve her particular problems in her particular terms. I feel entirely confident that her house will be the best house we have ever done. I have felt this about every house we have ever designed, and no one seems to have been very disappointed.

Young men have frequently asked how they may get their work published, and, of course, one just can't rudely say that if it is good enough, or exotic enough, or sufficiently simple, or sufficiently complex, then there is no problem. For all the slick magazines' tendency to put out for public consumption only the more brash efforts, the more avant-garde articles, the magazines do exercise a reasonable discrimination about quality. They ride with each cliché and pot of cleverness, but they amend this just as adroitly by light criticism and the sudden elimination of that fashion from their pages. I care not what they publish so long as it represents the best work—the most imaginative, the most scholarly—or even just informative material, but I do resent all the mishmash of adulation and flattering language, the omniscient pronunciamentos, the wise words of these journalistic oracles. I do not want my parking garage, however romantic, likened to a "Roman Road" or my plain and simple factory to be called "Horizontal Gothic." The writer may do me justice by saying, "This is the house that Jack built—for Mr. Jones." The style of writing in architectural magazines has become quite as laboriously devious as the writings of art critics who bend hard to explain a painter's three swift strokes of green thrown across two brave blobs of red. Architecture is not something abstract; it is not nebulous; it is not tentative. It is accomplished by very much hard work.

Those who answered a check list several years ago may well have felt pride in the importance of their checking "Play golf with prospective clients," "Regularly attend service club meetings," "Hold position on chamber of commerce committees," "Make lectures to service clubs, women's groups, etc.," "Know my local, state, and national representatives," etc.; but I prefer my own kind of check list. I give many lectures, perhaps too many, for causes I believe in. I walk in the country and in every new town I visit in Europe, Mexico, and the United States. Mostly, I work—evenings and many holidays, as do my associates. When I am not working, I read. This reading is history of architecture and the other arts, history of religion and Western civilization, history of Texas and America. I have read every book on the architecture and art of Byzantium, on Moslem architecture, on the architecture of the Middle Ages, on the architecture of Latin America, that I could get or crowd into air flights and the late hours of night. Two of my associates read more. One reads while he eats and one while he waits for trains or planes. We are excited—that's the only word that describes our feelings—about our discoveries in books. When I am in Europe (and I have been most fortunate to go there fourteen times in six years), I ride buses, planes, trains, and automobiles to see our wonderful discoveries. I have crisscrossed England, southern France, northern Spain, and northern Italy over and over again. I have also spent time in Holland, Belgium, and the Scandinavian countries. I have felt ecstasy over seeing the great cathedral at Albi, because it was the subject of one of our serious studies. In its presence I felt quite humble. I have devoted hours to seeing Giselbertus' great sculpture at Autun. This could go on and on. I know the back streets of London better than the front streets of Houston, because I had seen the beauty of the good Queen Anne and Georgian buildings in books before my firsthand visits. Twenty times I have seen Egyptian and Syrian sculpture in the British Museum, and I will see them again. Since 1926, I have traveled on sideroads in Texas looking for the simple native houses— the log houses near Jasper, the Classic Revival houses from Austin eastward, the stone houses of the German towns in the hill country. I have been up and down the Rio Grande just looking and taking pictures. I have been to Victoria and Galveston to see the frilly houses of Saratoga Springs, the fine Victorian things in St. Louis and in Albany and Augusta, Georgia. These and a thousand other towns I have seen and read about and loved. I do not know where this leads or whether it soaks into our work, but it is the essence of my pleasure and all of my recreation. I do not aspire to be a Kenneth Conant, who knows most of the medieval work by the square foot and how and when it was built. I feel no desire to be an expert on the late nineteenth century, but I cherish the vigor of its builders.

There is time for some of this, but much more time is required for just work; and I am not the least disturbed that I don't want to play golf or bridge, that I don't want to hunt or fish. I have not and will not make social functions, or rig a fishing trip, or play golf, or drink beer or even champagne with anyone just to put myself closer to a "prospect." I believe that an architect who knows how much he should know, how much work is required to cover his limitations of talent, what great happiness is on the inside of creativity, and what pleasures are in all the related spheres can do little more than work and study. I have a very good time at what I do and stay busy and not very businesslike. What we do is limited by the boundaries of our several and our whole abilities and time, but it is done with absolutely consuming enthusiasm. I hope this same enthusiasm goes to the people for whom we build. I do not want to know "how to have a satisfied client." I want an ecstatic one.

I do not want our group to become school experts, laboratory experts, hospital experts, or house experts. I hope we may learn to approach each problem and opportunity with the resolve to put the client's needs first and to be ready to exert ourselves to meet any demand, so that we serve significantly and, as often as possible, design buildings of real beauty with a measure of originality that is purposeful and fitting. We strive scrupulously to avoid decorative fashions and to keep abreast of technical advancements and use them to the end that our work is entirely contemporary in engineering, erection, and material techniques. We study the construction of Romanesque, Gothic, Renaissance, and nineteenth-century buildings so that we may know better the sequence in the growth of systems and engineering that brings us to this day of great spans and heights, in order to make advantageous use of stressing, warping, precasting, and welding. With the knowledge and use of these techniques, we should be able to work in the real tradition of architecture and not find any necessity or desire to fling ourselves into the current parade of cleverness and playful, capital "D" design.

I have no time to discuss the importance of the architect as the logical man in the logical profession to speak loudly and consistently against the brutal destruction of the good things our forebears gave us. Nothing has been said about tribute to those who have made themselves very unpopular by publicly standing against the gobbling of parks and green areas everywhere by casually designed expressways, canals, and parking lots. Only those architects who conduct their practice as a business—as a routine promotion and production activity—and carefuly avoid controversy and debate can possibly remain entirely acceptable to everyone.

That I may proudly praise our city council (in San Antonio) for its attitude toward desegregation, its interest in the development and further beautification of our little downtown river, its growing interest in preservation of historic buildings, its vigorous program of urban renewal, and the support of fiestas and pageants is a strong source of satisfaction to me and my associates. When we must fight hard and spend money and endless days and weeks to oppose the cutting of trees, the destruction of a park or plaza for a parking lot, the expediency of "saving" land cost by setting an expressway through our great park and forested area, then the same men I previously praised for their better acts, must look upon us as obstructionists and non-conformists. The Chamber of Commerce—of which I am a member—is pleased to have my support in their splendid plan to expand our downtown parks and widen and improve our river walk area, but when I protest their support of the expressway through a campus and parks, they must find me an annoyance. They must set me up as a belligerent and controversial reactionary when I cry, "Wait, study this carefully, take time to be sure there isn't another way through a slum. Take time to be sure the extra money for a better right-of-way isn't cheap compared with the irreparable destruction of open areas. Think, worthy councilmen, how we will need this 'unused' land when our population has doubled."

During the last several years the A.I.A. has begun to take a strong position against this new urge to rip apart our cities and remove all native identity and character. Yet, sadly, most of the fighting, the serious concern, the study of alternate solutions, has been left to a few with courage and the willingness to be unpopular. The fight goes on around the world from San Antonio, to New York, London, Florence, and Milwaukee, and back again to Dallas. Architects must lead the fight and provide creative counsel and plans. May each of us with his particular ability join in the desperate fight to save our land from the reckless, the wilful, the selfish, the unimaginative, and the just plain ignorant vulgarians. One important thing an association, with the help of its membership, can and must do is work to achieve the significant and larger purpose of serving all people.

My rambling remarks have been intended as a plea that may be summed up in a good scholarly way by a quotation from a little book by Ralph Tubbs called, modestly enough, *An Englishman Builds*.

I refer to contact of the mind of the builder directly through the form of the building itself, not by association; there is no intent to add "human interest." The knowledge that the name of the man who directed operations during the building of Lichfield Cathedral was William de Ramessey adds no more to our real appreciation of this cathedral than we are helped to understand Beethoven's Ninth Symphony by the knowledge that he dedicated it to the King of Prussia. The building alone and the music alone convey to us something which could not be conveyed to us by any other means than by the building or the music.

Buildings appeal to us in different ways; our eyes may be delighted by the colour, texture or form; our intellect may be stimulated by the skillful use of materials or the brilliance of building techniques; or our sense of fitness may be impressed by the excellence of the building for its purpose. In each case, however, we see revealed to us something of the living man, for no architect can give his building a finer quality than exists in his own mind.

So may we look sharply to "quality," to the "joy of living," and to the fervent search for "knowledge."

Victor Gruen combines the activities of architect and planner: he regards himself as an environmental architect. From his offices in Los Angeles, New York, and Chicago, he directs his firm's activities both in the United States and abroad.

Mr. Gruen is interested in cities—in particular their core areas—and in the problems of the twentieth-century metropolis. He feels that architecture's most urgent mission today is "to convert chaos into order, change mechanization from a tyrant to a slave, and thus make a place for beauty where there is vulgarity and ugliness." He has expressed this philosophy emphatically in regional shopping centers in Detroit, Minneapolis, Chicago, Philadelphia, Albuquerque, and other cities. By making the shopping center more than just a "shopping" center, he has filled "that great unanswered need of suburbia for a crystallization point." This same idea of environmental design permeates all his work, including office buildings, apartment houses, and revitalization projects for numerous city cores.

Well known for his frequent articles in leading professional and general periodicals in this country and in Europe, Victor Gruen, in collaboration with economic consultant Larry Smith, is the author of *Shopping Towns U.S.A.* and is currently completing another book, "The Heart of Our Cities," dealing with urban diseases and their cure.

Mr. Gruen is honored especially for his design of towns and shopping centers.

Victor Gruen / Environmental Architecture

The term "people's architect" has been coined, it appears to me, to denote a special type of architect whose main interest and main activity is directed toward serving humanity. In coining this term, a distinction has been attempted between a "people's architect" and an "architect's architect." The latter term, then, is meant to apply to an architect who seeks self-expression above all, a man who is sometimes also referred to as a "form-giver" or a "prima ballerina," and who acts in a purely egotistical fashion as compared with the "modest, thoughtful people's architect," whose aspirations are only directed toward social betterment.

I am afraid that I can't quite agree that such a black and white picture exists. I believe that everybody who takes up the study and practice of architecture on the basis of a true inner compulsion (and that means that I except those who just want to take over their father's firm or who regard architecture as a short cut to a lucrative real estate business) is driven to his choice by a number of considerations. First, he is interested in the creative aspects of architecture, a profession which he hopes will give him a chance to translate thoughts into drawings and then into brick and mortar, steel and concrete. His great inner reward is derived from witnessing the utilization of the structure he has created and its contemplation by its users and the public. Inherent in this satisfaction is, of course, the desire for personal expression, something which is popularly referred to as artistic drive, but I don't see why this desire for self-expression should be assumed to be in conflict with the desire of serving people. Human welfare, after all, does not depend only on creating sanitary dwellings, efficient hospitals, or practical school rooms. It also entails the visual, spiritual, and psychological enjoyment that the creations of architecture can transmit.

Architecture is a many faceted activity. There are those who regard architecture as an art and those who feel it is a technique, others who regard it purely as a profession and still others who see in it a social service. All efforts to circumscribe the exact nature of architecture betray its complexity. Take the statement of Vitruvius, as adapted by Sir Henry Wotton in *Elements of Architecture*: "Well building hath three conditions: commodity, firmness, and delight." In order to satisfy the first of these conditions, the architect has to be a sociologist and economist. In order to live up to the second, he must be an engineer and an expert on construction matters. And in order to qualify for the third, he must be a creative artist. It is my belief that every sincere architect tries hard to live up to all three demands. He usually has a fourth problem if he wasn't born a millionaire or didn't marry a millionaire's daughter, and that is to earn enough money to keep alive and to meet the payroll of his staff.

Depending on background, education, and temperament, I am sure that there are differences among individual architects concerning the emphasis placed on each of Vitrivius' three criteria. As long as there is striving to live up to all three demands, even though with differing emphasis, the title "architect" is fully deserved. If, however, one or more of the three ideal aims of architecture are completely disregarded or if the fourth one that I mentioned, namely, monetary return, becomes the principal driving force, then the title, even if recognized by registration, is misapplied. If a man worries only about firmness, then he is an engineer. If he is concerned only with delight, then he is a sculptor working on an unusually large scale. If it is only commodity that he is trying to achieve, then he may be a sociologist or industrial designer. And if monetary return is his main concern, then he is simply a businessman who might just as well, and probably more successfully, have devoted himself to the ready-to-wear business.

I believe that the graduation of emphasis concerning commodity, firmness, and delight should be influenced not only by the personal preference of the architect but also and to a high degree by the needs and requirements of society within a given time period. I further believe that the term commodity should not be related just to the needs of a single individual or group of individuals but to communities, towns, cities, regions, countries, and mankind as a whole.

We are living in an era of rapid and revolutionary change. This dynamic pattern of our times applies to progress in science and to stormy development in technology and in sociology. The physical expressions of our man-made and man-influenced environment have not been able to keep pace with the rapid changes brought about by science, technology, and social patterns. In our physical environment we have dealt with these changes over the last thirty to forty years by stop-gap measures, improvisation, or just by letting things drift, with the result that urban areas have been eroded through the infiltration of hundreds of thousands of gasoline-driven vehicles and landscape has been converted into a suburban sprawl. Because we have in the best cases improvised and in the worst cases applied a laissez faire policy, unworkable patterns for human habitation, for work, and for all other human activities have emerged and we have been caught in a never ending rat race of FLIGHT and BLIGHT. Whenever we find that a particular area becomes, because of its poor functioning pattern and environmental conditions, unworkable and uninhabitable, we escape from it and start just as planlessly somewhere else only to find after a comparatively short time-interval that we have created anew the same unbearable conditions and the same necessity for flight.

Because we have neglected "commodity" as far as our public environment is concerned, though we have been quite successful in achieving private commodity, we have destroyed the urban values of our cities. Cities have always been regarded as the proudest achievement of human civilization. They have since time immemorial fulfilled many functions, but their most significant role has always been to make possible easy and intimate human communication and the fruitful exchange of ideas and goods. Cities achieved these aims by constituting compact organisms that provided in a tightly woven fabric the greatest variety of settings for all types of human activity—residences and working places, shops and churches, theaters and civic institutions, social and entertainment organizations, education and business headquarters.

Our cities today with some very minor exceptions don't fulfil their original purposes any longer. We have quite mistakenly attempted to adjust our cities and their physical structure to certain technological developments, in particular to the motor car as a means of mass transportation, and in the procedure have robbed them of their most significant characteristic—that of compactness and variety. We have torn apart the tightly woven urban fabric to make space for the concrete ribbons that automobiles need in order to move and for parking lots and garages that they need in order to rest. By allowing the dangers, fumes, and noises that vast hordes of automobiles create to infiltrate into the urban living room, we have driven out of that living room all of those who seek quietude, safety, and better air. We have made refugees of millions of urbanites, driving them out into the outlying areas of suburbia and the metropolitan region. The flight of the residents was then followed by the merchants, by business enterprises of all types, until the core areas of our cities became working quarters only for civic and business administration and certain professions that depended directly on these institutions. No wonder that most of our city centers are today deteriorating physically and economically, alive only during working hours and veritable ghost towns in the evenings and on holidays. The panicky, disorderly flight into suburbia has created an anarchic physical environment there as well, beset by traffic problems, contamination of air and water, and a severe lack of cultural and social amenities.

The main characteristic of the man-made and man-influenced environment in our times is therefore utter disorder; the major need of our times is to re-establish an orderly public environment as a basis for the regeneration of human civilization and human culture. The establishment of order and workable patterns for a truly humane urban environment is most decisively the role of architecture. If the products of architecture are to be meaningful, they must have a chance to be contemplated in order to be enjoyed. In our presently existing anarchic public environment, there is little chance for this contemplation. The architect of even the most brilliantly designed single structure within a disorderly environment cannot help but be overcome by a sense of frustration because of the nullification of his efforts by the hostility of the surroundings of his building. His structure cannot be contemplated because of the traffic mess surrounding it. It is usually observed by only three people—the architect, who approaches it in the early morning hours when without danger of being run over he can appreciate its qualities from the best viewpoint and still remain alive, the architectural photographer, who can catch the building from the right angle by carefully scheduling his picture-taking time, and the architectural critic, who in discussing the building divorces it in his mind from all disturbing outside influences.

This is why I feel that the conditions of our time make it necessary for the architect to concern himself not just with private commodity but with public commodity. This is why I feel that it is the architect's responsibility today to become an "environmental architect," an architect who concerns himself not just with the individual structure but with the total man-made and man-influenced environment. If architecture is ever again to become a successful creative effort with the aim of causing delight, then its expressions must be communicable to those who are to experience it. Architecture set into a chaotic physical environment has about as much chance to stir the emotions as a violin concerto has on the runway of a jet airport. If we architects don't wish to experience total frustration, then we must be the creators and generators of that basic order that will give to the individual building or to a group of buildings a chance to fulfil its function. Our clients, after all, are no longer the ones who in times past held a disproportionate share of wealth and power. No longer are we expected to design only palaces, temples, churches, monuments, and castles. Our client has become society as a whole. In order to satisfy that client, we have to start from the foundation, from the ground up, by creating a healthy, livable, enjoyable, "delightful" urban environment.

In these times of specialization, of course, there are those who will tell us that concern with the environment is none of the architect's business, that activity in these areas is reserved to the planner, the traffic engineer, the economist, the sociologist, the politician, the administrator, and so on. There is no doubt that all of these people have to make important contributions, but there is also no doubt that their efforts will be fruitful only if leadership and co-ordination is provided. There is only one profession trained to think in three-dimensional terms, which is able to fulfil this leadership and co-ordinating role: the architect. The original Greek term *architekton* had the meaning "master mason" or "master builder." The person who held this title sited buildings; he was a technician, a painter, and a sculptor; and in addition he assumed the leadership of a team of draftsmen, artists, artisans, technicians, and laborers.

If architecture is ever to be enabled again to provide commodity, firmness, and delight, then it will have to assume fully and unstintingly this leadership role. Faced as we are with an extremely complex society and technology, the task has become, of course, a very complicated one. The team of specialists with whom the architect has to co-operate has become an army. The knowledge which the architect has to acquire in order to equip himself properly for his co-ordinating role has grown tremendously. Yet, if we architects truly want to deserve the flattering term "people's architect," we will have to become shapers of the environment. Only if we succeed in this task, will we be able to bring about an urban renaissance and with it a renaissance of architecture as the art, science, and profession of creating "commodity, firmness, and delight."

Ieoh Ming Pei, a partner of I. M. Pei & Associates, Architects and Planners, was born in Canton, China, on April 26, 1917. In 1935 he came to the United States to enter the Massachusetts Institute of Technology, from which he received his Bachelor of Architecture degree in 1939. He became a naturalized citizen of the United States in November of 1954.

He received his Master of Architecture degree from the Harvard Graduate School of Design in 1946, and was on the faculty from 1945 to 1948. He was appointed assistant professor in 1946. The M.I.T. Traveling Fellowship was awarded him in 1940, and the Harvard Wheelwright Fellowship in 1951. A member of the Visiting Committee of the Harvard Graduate School of Design from 1958 to 1963, he has also served on the Visiting Committee on Architectural Education of M.I.T., from 1956 to 1959, and on the Federal Housing Authority Multifamily Housing Committee, from 1958 to 1960.

Mr. Pei was elected a member of the Department of Art of the National Institute of Arts and Letters in February of 1963. He was also elected an associate member of the National Academy of Design in April of 1963.

Mr. Pei was the 1961 recipient of the Arnold Brunner Award given by the National Institute of Arts and Letters for excellence in the field of architecture, and in 1963 he was awarded the Medal of Honor by the New York chapter of the American Institute of Architects. In 1964 he was elected to membership in the College of Fellows in the AIA for achievement in design.

It is for his design of multistory buildings that Rice University honors I. M. Pei.

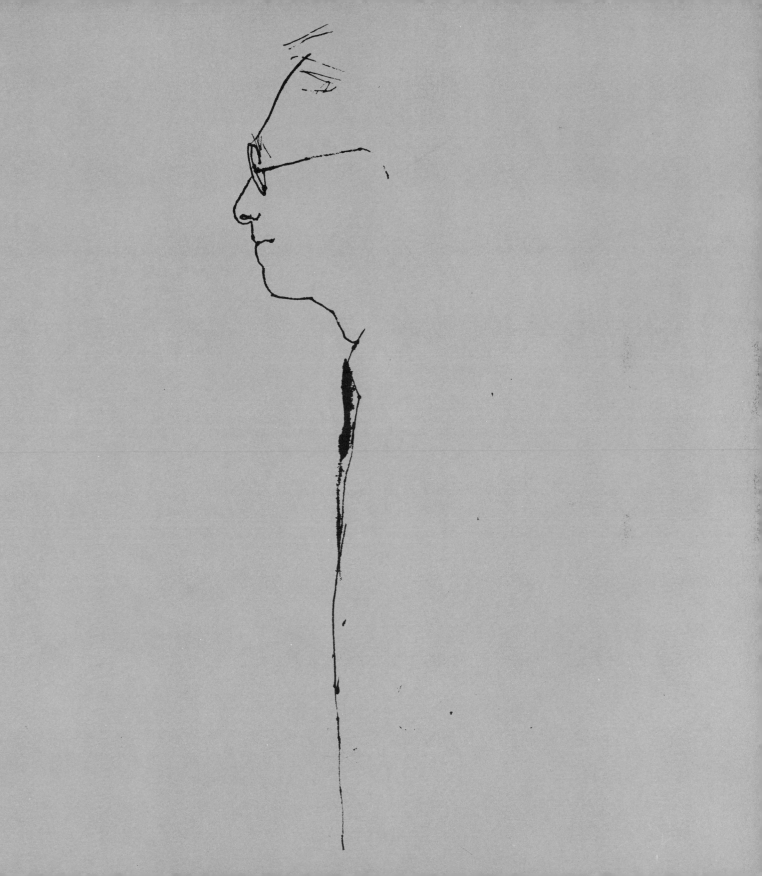

I. M. Pei / The Nature of Urban Spaces

The ancient philosopher Lao-tse once remarked that the essence of a vessel is its emptiness. A city, in a sense, is a vessel, too—a container for people and for life. A city's essence, like a vessel's, also lies in its voids—its public spaces.

Most of us think of a city as a group of buildings. Yet we know from personal experience that the real flavor of a city comes from its spaces—its streets, squares, rivers, and parks. We notice that the quality of life pursued in any space has much to do with its design. Poorly designed spaces inhibit life and movement. Well-designed ones raise the ordinary rituals of life to a high level of intensity and purpose. The conclusion seems to be that a city, so far from being a cluster of buildings, is actually a sequence of spaces enclosed and defined by buildings. The thought may seem strange; yet it is, in fact, the very essence of urban design. And every architect who enters this interesting field will soon find himself designing buildings and spaces as a single entity. More often than not, he is likely to be more concerned with voids rather than volumes, surfaces rather than solids, for the character of a space is determined by its bounding surfaces—the façades of the enclosing buildings.

In attempting to speculate on the nature of urban spaces, I shall limit myself to the aesthetic factors. It must be taken for granted that no urban space can ever be successful, however well designed, unless there is a social, economic, and political reason for its existence.

The first factor, and perhaps the most important of them all, is scale. To develop a space to its highest intensity, the scale of the façades that enclose it must match the scale of the space itself. A large square needs important, monumental structures around it. A narrow street should have small-scale buildings along it. The idea seems self-evident, except that scale is often confused with sheer size; they are by no means the same thing. The Piazza San Pietro in Rome is an enormous oval of 650 feet by 500 feet, whereas the surrounding colonnade is only 65 feet high. Yet it is one of the world's most majestic urban spaces. The reason is that Bernini's colonnade, despite its modest over-all height, is conceived on a huge scale. Scale here alone sustains an enormous space.

A second and a far more complex factor is the shape and extent of the space's bounding surface. To be felt as a space, an open area, as a general rule, needs to have enough of an enclosure to define it. If there are too many openings or too many interruptions in the surrounding façade, the space will drain away. In Venice the designers of the Piazza San Marco felt the need for enclosure so strongly that they finished off the surrounding buildings on three sides with an unbroken façade and even forced approaching streets and alleys to enter through arcades so as not to interrupt the continuous fabric of the architectural envelope. This piazza is one of the most extreme examples of complete enclosure that comes readily to mind. The continuous buildings around it are as solid as anyone could wish. Yet they are experienced as surfaces and are meant to be. It may be surprising that a space as large as the piazza could be so intimate; but the almost total enclosure makes it so. The more completely a space is enclosed, the smaller, tighter, and more intense the space appears to be.

Applying this principle to present-day planning experiences, we may observe that long-slab buildings enclose a space more completely than point buildings or towers. In the Kips Bay apartment project in Manhattan, a pair of twenty-story, 400-foot-long buildings stand parallel to each other. A distance of about 300 feet separates them. It might have been more economical of available space to build them closer together. But this space, though open at its two distant ends, is nevertheless substantially enclosed by the length and the bulk of the two buildings and therefore seems smaller and more confined than its actual dimensions would suggest. In the Society Hill section of Philadelphia, on the other hand, three tall apartment towers stand grouped around an open space that is a mere 180 feet across. There is no sense of confinement here even though the buildings rise over it to a height of thirty-one stories. The reason is that the space is far less enclosed than at Kips Bay. There are wide gaps between the towers through which the space can leak out into the beyond. This leakage reduces the intensity of the space. The Society Hill towers could have been considerably higher and a pedestrian on the ground would not feel any additional sense of confinement as he walks between them. To express it differently, the space between the Society Hill towers is actually a fluid space: the stream of movement flows into it, around it, and out again with ease. The space at Kips Bay lacks this implied movement. It is more intense. It is static and therefore needs more room to breathe.

Closely related to the scale and extent of the architectural envelopment is a third factor—the formality of its design. A space gains immensely in intensity, in grandeur, and in importance when the buildings around it are conceived within the framework of a single formal design. The Piazza San Pietro again furnishes a striking example. Others are the Place Vendôme in Paris, the Piazza San Carlo in Turin, and the Place Stanislaus in Nancy, where the formal symmetry of the buildings, the strict axial arrangement, and the rhythmical repetition of motifs raise the quality of the space to a level of ceremonial impressiveness.

Here, it should be mentioned that the three-dimensional accents within a space often play an important part. Paris' Place de la Concorde is almost unique in that, with the exception of the Madeleine block, it has virtually no surrounding façade at all. Yet it is clear, intense, and articulate, and the chief reason for this, I believe, lies in its interior accents—its two great fountains and obelisk, lanterns, and paving patterns—which actually create a form of their own. In the Piazza del Popolo in Rome, the one central obelisk, together with Rainaldi's twin churches opposite the Porta, performs a similarly effective function.

A fourth factor in the design of open spaces is one that is imposed by nature rather than by man. It is the element of light. Everyone knows that light and climate affect architecture; for instance, large windows in the North let in the weak sun and little windows in the South keep out the glare. But light also affects our experience of spaces. The bright sun of Mediterranean lands tends to make spaces look bigger than they really are. The grey light of the North makes them look smaller. The alleys of Mykonos, for example, seem far more spacious than the streets of Chartres. Differences in the scale of buildings undoubtedly play a part, but the quality of light remains the determining factor. The Grande Place in Brussels, with its dark buildings under the Northern sun, looks relatively small; Constitution Square in Athens, though similar in scale, looks immense in the blinding Aegean light.

Up to this point, I have discussed urban spaces as if they were isolated entities, separate and self-contained. But the effectiveness of a space also depends upon its neighbors. When we walk through a city, we actually experience a series of spaces in sequence; and the impact of any particular space, whether a street, a passageway, or a square, is multiplied many times over by what we have already seen before and by what follows afterward. The classic example is in Nancy, where three spaces are lined up along a single axis. The two terminal spaces are broad, monumental, and ceremonial squares; the connecting space is long, narrow, residential, and divided by rows of trees. The effectiveness of the two ceremonial squares is tremendously heightened by the change of pace provided by the central residential space, the Place Carriere, which is designed on a far smaller scale. Conversely, the residential space seems all the more intimate and human because of the contrast it affords to the large scale of the two terminal squares. Each reinforces the character of the other when experienced in sequence. Architects, then, must think of urban spaces as a sequential experience and strive to orchestrate them into an effective ensemble. They should alternate wide spaces with narrow ones, constriction with expansion, concealment with revelation, so that each space intensifies and dramatizes its neighbors until, as a result, the whole becomes something greater than the sum of its parts. In this, I think, we become close at last to part of the secret of a city's visual quality.

These are a few of the factors that seem to me relevant to the aesthetics of urban spaces. They are hard to rationalize and harder yet to measure, for urban space is a medium that still remains elusive, immeasurable, and often more successfully approached by intuition than by logic and mathematics. Sometimes, as if to mock our efforts to understand, a successful space will result from a wilful breaking of all the rules. I am always astonished by Rockefeller Plaza, a space that by all rights ought to be oppressive because of its comparatively small area, the almost total enclosure, the immense scale and size of the surrounding buildings and the deep shadows in which most of it lies throughout the year. And yet Rockefeller Plaza is one of the most exciting urban spaces I know of. One can only speculate. Most beautiful things, they say, contain within them some exaggeration. Can it be that in New York, whose special beauty rests in the spectacular, in the exaggerated, a space as far-fetched and beyond all bounds as Rockefeller Plaza is the only kind that can capture the spirit of the city and intensify it?

Baffling questions like this remind us how little we really know about urban design. The elementary principles I have touched on here were once common architectural currency during the Baroque period. It is no accident that I have drawn most of my illustrations from that extraordinary era. From Bernini to Gabriel, the great Baroque space-makers translated order and discipline, the powerful instincts of their age, into the fabric of their cities. They mirrored the strict hierarchy of life in architectural subordination and emphasis. They expressed the ceremonial spirit of the age—its endless processions, parades, and spectacles, secular and religious—in elaborate and formally planned public spaces that heightened its solemnity. The Baroque sense of the theatrical became, in the hands of these architects, a dramatic sequence of spaces. And the delight in movement was satisfied by great boulevards carefully framed to lead body and eye onward with irresistible momentum.

Order, drama, movement—these were the impulses that produced the majestic plans and spaces of the great Baroque cities of the Continent. To these England added an important ingredient—the human touch. In England the ceremonial and public aspect of cities was balanced by the domestic and private. England's first contribution to urbanism was Inigo Jones's Covent Garden which was designed in the classical manner. Subsequent to this, trees and greenery began to invade English public spaces. The architectural setting followed suit with small-scale residential façades in place of the exclusively monumental ones. The Royal Crescent at Bath forms an immense elliptical arc of almost 600 feet in length, yet the scale of the continuous façade and the corresponding intimacy of the tree-filled park make the ensemble seem warmly personal. The Baroque sense of order is not once compromised. Nevertheless, the human scale asserts itself.

Today in America we stand on the threshhold of an exciting era of urban planning and development. The public mind, now familiar with the splendors of Europe's cities, looks for similar beauty, spirit, and vitality in its own. Ever since the introduction of the National Housing Act of 1949, and particularly since its amendment in 1954, large segments of cities are being replanned and rebuilt. Architects are once again confronted by the challenge and the opportunity to create the kind of urban spaces that mirror our lives and aspirations.

In searching for guidance, it is only natural that we should turn to the Baroque planners. Admittedly, they gave scant attention to satisfying the social needs we consider important in our time. The social relationships for which they sought to provide a framework are not, despite the passage of centuries, so very different from our own. We, too, need order and discipline in our cities. We, too, need to provide for movement, though of a different sort. We also need a sense of drama to provide for a ceremonial side of life that seems to be re-emerging. And yet we have forgotten the very fundamentals on which the Baroque planners built their cities. To plan wisely and well, we must first relearn what they knew. This does not bind us to a slavish imitation. Much has changed since then. The high population density of most of our cities rules out the leisurely residential solution reached by the English planners, at least in strictly urban areas. And the development of new building techniques and materials has opened up new opportunities for exciting urban designs far beyond the reach or imagination of the Baroque masters. But the fundamental discoveries they made about the nature and aesthetics of urban spaces are as valid today as then. In this respect, the careful study of Baroque cities is still deeply rewarding and is likely to remain so for years to come.

Vernon DeMars

Vernon DeMars combines both the teaching and the practice of architecture: he is presently a professor of architecture at the University of California at Berkeley.

Mr. DeMars has been designing housing and communities for many years and has never felt the need to restrict himself to "traditional" solutions. His early works include over forty migratory labor camps and rural communities throughout the western states. He has been a planning and housing consultant to several governmental agencies. More recent communities of his design include Easter Hill Village and "The Plaza" in Richmond, California; Capitol Towers in Sacramento; and the Golden Gateway redevelopment project in San Francisco. Mr. DeMars feels that housing by its very nature forms "the background of the urban tapestry" and should complement the city as a whole. At the same time, the design of the communities must take into consideration the way the families that will use them want to live and need to live and ought to live. Both the community and the individual dwelling unit must be developed. The social implications of a design must be recognized. Cost is not a handicap but rather is accepted as one of the limitations inherent in the architect's work.

Related to the problem of communities is a special kind of community —the university campus. Mr. DeMars' recent design for the student center of the University of California at Berkeley demonstrates again his belief in the power that architecture and planning can exercise in forming a society.

Vernon DeMars has been honored by Rice University especially for his design of communities.

Vernon DeMars / People's Architecture: The Urban Environment

To be a "people's architect" should not prevent one from being an "architect's architect," but it often does. Perhaps all architects think of themselves as "people's architects." Even those who design to please no one but themselves may argue, not without reason, "Aren't we people?" But the title "people's architect" may suggest that "people" should be understood collectively, and many architects have designed structures for people in this sense. The distinction, I think, is whether the architect thinks of "the people" as a crowd—a kind of monolithic, centipede-like unity—or whether he can bring himself to worry about them as a collection of individuals. I like to think that the latter has been my approach.

There are many problems, in the practice of his art, that the architect can set himself today, though they are not as clear-cut as when I entered the profession back in the thirties. There was only one problem then: to carry out the architectural revolution—to wean both public and profession from a grab bag of styles and to persuade them to accept the inevitability of a new architecture, a new architecture deriving its very form and aesthetics from the direct response and simplest solution to the needs of a problem. I am not so sure that we were wrong either, but it was almost too easy. There were few real battles in this revolution. Little pockets of resistance were simply bypassed or ignored; and either they dried up for lack of supplies—starved out, so to speak—or the resistors came over and joined the revolution, some of them changing colors with no trouble at all, others trying hard but never quite understanding what it was all about— going through the motions, acting as they thought they were expected to, but rather yearning for the good old days, which now had passed beyond recall.

So, in a few short years it was all over. No more Corinthian capitals carved by imported Italian stonemasons; no more Doric columns of solid granite hollowed out from end to end to provide for (and to conceal) the steel column needed to support the ten-story building above (this really happened in San Francisco). No more yard after yard of eggs and darts in pressed tin for the useless cornices high above the street. All this had to go—and high time, too. Except for other architects, none of this really had any meaning; for the public, familiarity bred either comfortable complacency among the haves, contempt among the have-nots, or indifference. Besides, it all cost too much.

So the new architecture had a certain appeal. Of course, clients needed assurance that they were not going to get the sort of buildings being designed by those foreigners in France and Germany (which we secretly admired). No, this was to be an American architecture, or at least an international architecture, not merely a foreign one. We talked; we pleaded; we put together exhibits; we even managed to build a few little buildings to show what we meant. Till finally we began hearing from all sides, "All right, all right, ALL RIGHT! Give us this new architecture; it's all we can afford anyway (I need a $20,000 house, and since the most I can afford is $10,000, you're my man.") So we gave them the new architecture stripped to fighting trim, no nonsense, utility is beauty, form follows function, less is more. And now they've had it, as the English say—a lot of it. And something seems to be lacking. Even those pressed-tin eggs and darts begin to look good again.

I am grateful, therefore, that some of our colleagues are exploring the very frontiers of aesthetic expression in the new architecture. And although they might protest that they do this with no less concern for function and clients' needs than the rest of us, the fact remains that the aesthetic rules of behavior that they are willing to obey are usually self-made and their preoccupation, more often than not, is heavily weighted on the side of the visual statement. If anything must give—and it almost always must—then function, logic, humanity, or economy gets the rap; architecture as sculpture must prevail. Now the rest of us who like to think that we worry in equal amounts about "firmness, commodity, and delight" are not disinterested in our own architecture as sculpture. Perhaps it's just that we don't expect to make it every time, for most architecture is much more than sculpture, and some of it isn't going to make good sculpture, at least not in the mode of the moment, whatever that may be. In a problem well solved, however, the aesthetics are by definition built in, and there is ultimately a pleasure, part sensual, part intellectual, which comes with experiencing the rightness of a solution. If this is so in single works of architecture, it is even more so in the collective architecture of the townscape. In fact, the whole question of assessing beauty or ugliness in environmental situations becomes a matter of rightness or wrongness—of appropriateness—rather than of concise formal relationships.

There are stirrings in the land suggesting that environment is not a simple thing to be designed with the finality of a footstool or a carport or a split-level ranch house. Jane Jacobs, in her book *Death and Life of Great American Cities*, questions whether cities can or should be designed at all, at least not, in her thinking, by a generation of planners and architects who espouse the theories of virtually everybody from Ebenezer Howard through Corbusier to Mumford. Miss Jacobs lays it on the line: "When we deal with cities we are dealing with life at its most complex and intense. Because this is so, there is a basic aesthetic limitation on what can be done with cities: *A city cannot be a work of art.*" Although she concedes that art is needed in the arrangement of cities and in a host of things that illumine life, she continues: "To approach a city, or even a city neighborhood, as if it were a larger architectural problem, capable of being given order by converting it into a disciplined work of art is to make the mistake of attempting to substitute art for life."

There are some deep and disturbing ideas here, for have we not all had the experience of disappointment, emptiness, and boredom in great designed pieces of environment, from shopping centers to housing projects, that have been produced by some of our most talented architects? And what are the urban environments that do delight us? Why, usually the seemingly unplanned situations: the free-for-all of San Francisco's North Beach or New York's Greenwich Village area. It's a poor city, indeed, that does not have some counterpart of these. Yet, is "unplanned" the word? Few human activities take place without planning, and the planning of these areas must have been good—that is, *right* for the situation. But most likely, the planning consisted of a whole collection of little plans, all sensitively solving the little problems and coming up with a collectively right solution for the whole thing. Now it is true that when you experience these solutions they form an entirely different kind of visual composition from the "big design" of the Architect and Planner—much closer to the way our sister arts, from painting to music to literature, put things together today, midway in the twentieth century. Aren't there some lessons for us here?

Miss Jacob's thesis should give us pause. Granted her bias: she likes big cities, and the "sidewalks of New York" are her answer to almost too many of our problems—too many, since they are unique to New York, as unique as canals to Venice or pueblos to New Mexico. Yet, all too often, we continue to lean on the stereotypes of our urban theorists rather than seek in the problem itself a solution based on its own terms. Well, suppose we take that route and go to the problem itself. The architect still must act. He must make a host of design decisions, all colored by his approach, bias, analysis, and understanding of the problem.

Remember that both Miss Jacobs and I are talking about architecture taken collectively, and I am talking particularly about the problem of *designing* for collective architecture; and there's the rub. Can it be done? What is involved? How do we go about it? This, then, is really the subject of this essay for in all of my discussion I assume that a functional solution provides the underlying validity for whatever we are considering. And to me "functional" includes meeting and dealing with the social problems. But, granting all this how will it look? How will we react to it? We all know of "functional" solutions that are despised because they lack delight and, on the other hand, structures of charm and beauty that are forgiven some failure of function. Since, however, it is the very role and duty of the architect to provide both, why should we settle for less?

Let us consider first the "residential texture" of the urban fabric. I'd rather call it that than "housing," since housing seems to mean "projects" and Miss Jacobs and I are both against "projects." I'm against them because they are patches in the fabric that seldom match the goods, whereas it should be possible, where appropriate, to mend a worn-out spot in a way that barely shows or even in such a way that the whole thing looks better than before. All very well. But what if the architect must do a new development—

how is he not to do a "project"? First, he must want not to do it, since a
project is the easy way, for everyone from the banker and the builder and
the FHA to the architect himself if he is lazy or arrogant or merely incom-
petent. The project designs faster, builds faster, and works just dandy for
everyone except the people who have to live in it. And what is the antidote?
Miss Jacobs and I both agree on this one: It is diversity! Diversity in everything possible, from a wide range of dwelling types to all kinds of so-called
non-conforming uses that people need in everyday life—like a little corner
grocery if it can possibly support itself. "Diversity" implies apartments mixed
into generally single-family neighborhoods. Why? So grandma can live with
independence a few doors away but within easy proximity for everything from
emergencies to baby-sitting. So the newlyweds could, if they wanted to, rent
for a while near home, or in a new neighborhood to try it out before settling
down there. Now this means different types of buildings in close proximity
(almost as in real life, incidentally), and it poses interesting design problems and even more interesting opportunities for compositions of visual interest. "Diversity" implies a range of income levels and some range of social
interest and orientation. Back in 1943, Miles Colean, then assistant com-
missioner of the FHA, wrote in *Architectural Forum*:

There seems to be no sound reason why a neighborhood should contain exclusively one type of housing, one level of density, or one narrowly restricted
group of residents. The tendency toward what FHA refers to as homogeneity may
be overplayed whether it be in the types of houses or the incomes of their occu-
pants, to the disadvantage of neighborhood stability and a democratic way of life.
. . . Diversity, of course, can, like uniformity, be carried too far. We have to recognize again that we are dealing with people who have preferences and prejudices
as to the people around them. To the extent that such attitudes exist, they are

facts that must be taken into account by the planner. The difficulty is knowing positively to what extent they are facts, rather than something the planner himself takes for granted, and to what extent and through what means they might be successfully overcome should he have good cause for doing so. Here we need more enlightenment and perhaps greater willingness to experiment (Vol. LXXVIII [February, 1943], p. 94).

To which I can only add, Amen.

Twenty years have passed since that was written, and some of these experiments have been made, though the most spectacular ones are not in this country where they really should have taken place first. I refer, of course, to the New Towns in England and Sweden, which carry out Colean's prescription with dramatic if controversial results.

Still, to the architect, "diversity" is only the framework that presents him with design problems. How to deal with diverse uses? How to deal with the inevitable and necessary repetition of uses? What price variety? A special problem of today is the aesthetics of repetition under mass production. There is a vast difference between handmade objects that might be *called* identical and the products of machines that *are* identical. The first, whether wine flasks, baskets, ceramics, or stone houses with tile roofs, all have subtle differences and irregularities that allow identification. The machine product is terrifying in its uniformity. It must therefore be used only where this quality is a virtue. We cannot use the harmonious beauty of the similar tiled-roof dwellings of an Italian hill town to defend the deadly repetition of the identically fabricated houses of a merchant builder.

It has always been a temptation to plead for industrialized housing production by comparing houses with automobiles. A further argument has been that although automobiles from an assembly line are identical people don't seem to mind. These theorists overlook the fact that the products of many companies are scrambled together in the natural environment of the auto, whether parked or in motion. The tract house has been left on the assembly line right where it was built.

The desire for personal identification with automobile, home, fountain pen, or swimming trunks is so basic as to be almost biological. This need is even found among birds and animals, and it is not a question of legal ownership. Rent a bicycle for a day or so, and pretty soon you begin to recognize little endearing quirks and qualities that make it your own. You almost say good-by with a twinge when you turn it in. A house must find some way to differ from its neighbor, however subtly. Finding two identical cars together, in make, year, and color, is so unusual as to cause comment when it occurs. If it did occur frequently, measures from ingenious to drastic would be taken to modify the situation. The auto is in truth one of the most successfully industrialized products. I believe the variety of autos seen on the average street is sufficient to satisfy our demands for interest, identification, and personal expression. The factors at work are completely natural and organic—different types, makes, designs, colors, ages, finishes. The plans are the same for the most part—four wheels, seats front and back. This gives unity and harmony. Can we do as well with houses? Of course, furniture and clothes are also mass-produced. One seldom meets a man with the same suit (yet all are the same). When a woman meets another with the identical hat—well, it is one of the oldest jokes. Here we have mapped out the limits of expectancy in the average person concerning individuality and variety within a certain framework.

There is, however, a special phenomenon in architecture through which repetition develops added aesthetic impact up to a point. Repeated elements—arches, columns, windows—are the basic materials of design. Repeated entities, that is, whole buildings, are heady stuff and were used with caution by the ancients: the twin churches on the Piazza del Populo in Rome; the more modern twin temples at Potsdammer Platz in Berlin. Closer still to our time is the pair of apartment houses in Zurich designed by Alfred Roth and Marcel Breuer, who, incidentally, had planned to include a third. These examples all have in common the fact that the repeated architectural entity is in itself a strong, completely organized, finished statement, not one of a series that would be incomplete without the others.

Other than in housing, the doubled or tripled building is a rarity. However, from earliest times, dwellings as entities have been repeated, but with two quite different approaches. The first approach uses repetition to form larger compositions, as in the façades of the Place Royale in Paris or in the crescents and circuses at Bath, where side-by-side dwellings are joined so that they look like palaces—and for exactly that reason. In the second approach, dwellings are repeated without any expectation that they will form a composition at all, though they often do. Examples are the town houses of Bloomsbury in London or similar ones in Philadelphia or Georgetown. There was probably little question with either of these approaches of trying to achieve variety. In the first case, builders were trying to construct bigger and more impressive unities to set apart the aristocracy from the *hoi polloi*, who had all the variety then. In the second case, the eighteenth-century houses of Georgetown and Bloomsbury were built by speculators who were seldom able to get more than a half-dozen houses built in a row at one time anyway. The resulting subtle changes of minor detail from one group to the next is one of the delights of that housing type. Today, however, we can easily build hundreds of identical houses and often do. Sometimes this is sheer "public be damned," but it also may be the result of aesthetic conviction, as in the case of the Geneva Terrace houses of Joseph Eichler in San Francisco. Conviction, however, is not a guarantee against error.

Repetition, then, is a strong and permissible design device, but it must not be taken for granted. It is not the automatic way to successful urban composition; on the other hand, it should not be ruled out by the designer who is overzealous for variety.

Now, let us turn to those other elements that make up a city: the services, shops, recreation areas, and institutions. A host of new questions confronts us. What architectural character should these facilities exhibit? Should they blend with the housing? Should they contrast? The same old questions of variety and interest still prevail, but in a different framework. What of repetition now? of unity? of scale? Can there be an aesthetic equivalent of time in urban compositions? This is not a question of synthetic aging but of a purposeful attempt to make compositions with the scale and change of pace found naturally in old streets that have witnessed changes in use for generations. Nor is it a matter of some new eclecticism or other artificial approach. It is a matter of scale, of design invention—variations on a theme, perhaps— all done with strength and conviction. Gordon Cullen in his book *Townscape* shows the way.

Let us say we are considering the town center of a new town, or of an old town, for that matter, if it doesn't have a really satisfactory center now. Of course, the second case may be too easy, for a kind of life already exists there, even if the place isn't "jumping," and the existing problems lend hints for solutions. Such a town is often called "sick" by the planners. Here the good architect may serve a role from family doctor to plastic surgeon, and the bad one from quack to butcher. The problem of the entirely new center, however, is something else again. How can we put the breath of life into something we might describe as "instant city"? The large-scale enterprise implied by such a problem is not uncommon today. The vast regional shopping centers or certain of the urban renewal projects are examples that raise these issues. Architects are also being called on to master plan, lay out, and design new universities with the scale and population of a small city. Is there any way to heed Jane Jacobs' warning that a "city cannot be a work of art" and still perform a task and serve a need that society has set before us? I must think there is, or I wouldn't have opened this Pandora's box.

I suppose my answer is still "diversity," but new problems arise, and the issues are more highly charged than in the case of housing. Now we are getting into Architecture with a capital "A." You see, many of us feel that housing, or "the residential texture of the city," should be just that—a texture, a background interesting enough close up, but taken as a whole, a background for other things, things of shared community interest such as churches, schools, civic halls, and cultural and even business institutions. These are all more appropriate as focal points of community identification than housing. Buildings of this sort will appropriately be designed as the entities they are, and even Miss Jacobs will grant them leave to be a work of art if they can make it. But what if we have a group of some sort? a civic center? a cultural center? Miss Jacobs has an answer to that one. She wouldn't have them. They would be broken up and dispersed where their separate elements would become focal points and interest-generators in different parts of the city. Still, there are, and there are going to be, certain justifiable subgroupings of buildings. A city college might be one. Is unity desirable in such a case? If so, how then to achieve it? One way, of course, is to have only one architect; but that shouldn't be the only way. Besides, politics may not allow it. So we will have several architects. Will they all be willing to play the same tune?

There are, of course, several ways to play it. Architecture has been called frozen music. This image may help our analysis. The single building, modest in scope and scale, is the solo performance, unaccompanied, I suppose. The more ambitious single building, where one can still perceive and appreciate all its parts, is the string quartet (in which one can do the same). The highly unified group of buildings by one architect is like plain song, or the Gregorian chant, in which a group sings the same melody in unison. Such a building group is Saarinen's General Motors Research Center near Detroit or Mies van der Rohe's Illinois Institute of Technology buildings, or perhaps, an even more apt illustration, last year's top prize winner of the American Institute of Architects—Ernest Kump's Foothill College near San Jose, California. The unison approach has tremendous initial impact. It is immediately understandable. It is inherently non-confusing and therefore offers serenity. Its one lack may be in ability to sustain interest after a certain size has been reached, and of course, there is the question of how many of man's varied needs and activities can be made to fit into nearly identical shells, or conversely, whether this oversimplification does in fact express the reality of man's complex activities or even respect his ability to understand and enjoy complexity within order.

I feel the musical analogy continues to fit. Think next about the concept of harmony. Different instruments or voices accommodate to each other and, while making their own sound, combine to make a greater and unified total-ity, a blending in which the whole is definitely greater than the parts. Other periods of architecture have seemed more capable of achieving this than our own, for harmony in architecture as well as in music is only achieved by agreeing on some rules as to who is to play, when, at what tempo, and how loud; and of course, there must be some agreement as to what all of the par-ticipants want to come out at the end. As compositions become larger, they are inclined to become more complex—in music as well as architecture. Thus one group of voices sings in unison, contrasting with other groups or form-ing background support for the strong statement of the soloist. Past a certain scale, the work in music or architecture cannot be understood at first hearing (or seeing) but must be experienced serially and then repeated for fullest un-derstanding and enjoyment.

Another device bridging both these arts is counterpoint. It is concerned with the more general matter of approach in the creation of any work of art. A work can be composed in two ways: by unifying the component parts, colors, or sounds or by contrasting them—and the same artist may use either approach on different occasions or for different purposes. Counterpoint in-volves an entire melody or theme complete in itself played against another melody or theme complete in itself. The trained ear can hear both themes as well as the sound they make together. Of course, for this method to work harmoniously, which is the usual intent, there must be an internal structure or order that can provide the common denominator that will allow the themes to live together.

There are a host of other common terms in our two arts. And these are of more basic importance than as mere insights given by poetic imagery. The way the brain handles information that comes in from hearing and seeing is probably similar. Music depends on memory of what has just passed. The hearing of a great symphonic work depends on memory of something heard an hour earlier plus the additional memory of having heard it all before. So, too, with architecture. There is little impact or enjoyment to be obtained in the blink of an eye, scarcely more than that from an instant of sound cut off before and after a given moment. Architectural compositions—at least some kinds of them—must be experienced by passing through them and around them over a sufficient time for them to sink in and register.

There are one or two other items in the musical glossary that have their architectural counterparts. One of these is "disharmony." It is also called "discord" if you think of it as bad and to be avoided. If you want to use it on purpose in a composition, it is called "dissonance" or "atonality." In both architecture and music, this quality adds to the palette of expression by serving to heighten contrast. For another suggestion, try out the idea of jazz, or syncopation, or even the jam session, where accident or the mood of the moment calls for invention within a pre-established framework. These are widely accepted concepts in one art form. Can we say that they have no counterpart in another that is closely allied and similarly structured?

The concept of accident so pervades contemporary artistic expression that we must assess its role in architecture and the environment, since it is the strongest force determining the actual look of our cityscape—and sometimes the most creative and visually interesting force. In the complex network of chance that determines the final use of a property in the city—what client buys it, what store he decides to build, what architect he chooses—a change in any one factor produces a change in the end result. Therefore, one may well ask if there is any predictability at all in the look of a city. I think there is. One can try to make certain things happen that are considered desirable and try to control the ones that are not. But a planner's expectation must allow for a wide range of acceptable alternatives within the framework set up. Thus for the Diamond Heights development in San Francisco a wide range of housing types by different developers was proposed. The buildings that are beginning to appear may be unlike what we expected in one sense, yet exactly what we intended in another. That sounds as though we intended to be surprised by what might happen. Our expectation was rather that any of a number of things that might happen in detail would all be more or less equally acceptable.

Now let's consider a more concise building complex than housing, which I have already said should be a background, whose separate elements, therefore, have less need to be preordained by the planner. Are there just as many acceptable ways to do other types of building projects? Perhaps not as many. There are several right ways and surely some wrong ways. But certain kinds of building programs seem to produce buildings with a will of their own—a will to become something that seems to be almost independent of the architect —an inherent kind of inevitability that serves as guide for the designer, the tool, no doubt, that Lou Kahn speaks of when he asks a building's designer "what does the building want to be?"

Stanford Anderson, one of our students in Berkeley a few years back, investigated the basis of design decisions made by the contemporary architect. Tradition, he found, was enough for the Egyptian. God's omnipotence pervaded the Middle Ages. A new belief in man served the Renaissance. What do we believe in today? Anderson found in the philosophies of Alfred Whitehead and the late Albert Camus a basis of action for the architect, although it is significant that they were not speaking of the architect but of the creative person in general. Anderson transposes their message: "The only true life, the only true art, the only true architecture is one of realism. Like the true artist and rebel, the architect is firmly grounded in the 'real' world. *The architect seeks to give to reality that form which it seeks but has not!* He has a presentiment of an order that reality might have and seeks to make that order part of the real."

But in what way is this a guide to making design decisions concerning the environment? First, we do not accept the environment as it is. The chaos of much of our cityscape is not inevitable. It is really the expression of a need; in fact, it is a plaintive, sometimes raucous cry for help. The architect should answer that cry, not by the imposition of any preconceived ideas of order, but by giving to real situations the forms that they desire and need and even suggest.

Pietro Belluschi

Pietro Belluschi was born in Italy. He practiced architecture in Portland, Oregon, until, in 1951, he became dean of the School of Architecture and Planning at the Massachusetts Institute of Technology. In addition to his educational work, he still continues his personal practice.

Mr. Belluschi is an "artist-architect"; the fine arts have always been important to him. He is presently involved both in museum work and in various academies of art. This influence of the arts is reflected in the taste that he exercises, for example, in the careful proportioning and finishing of his designs. But more important is his idea that architecture is "the art and science of organizing space and relating it to man for his pleasure and comfort." The architect must come to terms with his contemporary environment—"a society conditioned by the machine and dominated by the desires of the common man"—for architecture is not an escape but an acceptance of the human condition. Only then can he hope to become creative, not in an academic sense, but rather as an interpreter of the new social order and as a prophet of his age.

Mr. Belluschi has designed several hundred commercial and residential buildings. He has served as consultant to the secretary of the Air Force on the new Air Academy and has been involved in the design of the Lincoln Center for the Performing Arts in New York City. He enjoys working with church architecture in particular, because this type of building lends itself so readily to the expression of human values and aspirations.

It is especially for his design of churches that Rice University has honored Pietro Belluschi.

What does it mean for architecture to serve the people? Taking a look at our environment, we might conclude that what we see is the result of well-intentioned builders doing their best to serve; but we would also know that architecture badly needs a whole range of creative efforts by all kinds of people to fulfil its civilizing role. To speak of this is not easy. One can become discouraged, even with the knowledge that our age is one of the most exciting in human history. The potential for good or evil, the very expectations for advancement in knowledge and exploration, have never been so great. Who will doubt that a great civilization is in the making? But the question remains: Will a great architecture emerge in its wake? And to this question I have no answer or any great message of hope; I am only able to echo all our doubts and hesitations. Perhaps we should ask what is meant by greatness when applied to a civilization or to architecture. In this we have only the great historical past as a standard of measurement, and history may be an inadequate gauge by which to measure our actions, to interpret new human needs, or to keep our minds creatively fluid in meeting them.

An eloquent case has been made that great architecture in our day can emerge only from acts of form-giving by an elite of artist-architects. Unfortunately, there are very few of them, and what they do is not always of enduring significance. It has also been said that this personal, in many cases even arrogant, approach to architecture has damaged rather than helped our environment. It would be easier to make a case for the need for wise technicians and honest draftsmen; unfortunately, if we can say that there are only a very few great artist-architects, it is also true that there are not enough competent and sensitive craftsmen. In the meanwhile, life has become immensely complicated. A prosperous society is imposing on our builders conditions of such variety and complexity that to find simple solutions or to develop a valid, commonly applicable aesthetic discipline seems like a hopeless task. In many ways the past still haunts and frustrates us. The sense of security afforded by the old traditional disciplines has gone; for some decades now we have had to develop our own discipline as we went along and as we searched for meaning and fulfilment.

Certainly, it is part of man's nature to wish to understand his condition and to find the means to adjust to it. He must find and believe in some kind of order that will allow him to survive. It is in this context that we must view the artist-innovator. We need him as a spearhead in the search for formal order, even when his forms are tentative or abstract. He teaches us to see; he searches for new meanings, for new songs to fit the words—and if the words are inadequate, he invents new ones. Through him, we gain that larger understanding needed to match the new dimensions of human knowledge. It may also be said that the form-giver, if sometimes pointing the way toward what we should do, may also reveal to us exactly what we should not do, so that we give up bad ideas with which we may have been toying.

It must be remembered that forms as well as ideas have a habit through age or usage of becoming crystallized, thereby losing strength and their ability to move us. We rely on the artist to make them free and eloquent again. This we must admit is a most difficult and dangerous task, particularly in a materialistic age when values continually shift and become confused; new, ephemeral philosophies arise and fast become obsolete; the taste-makers become bored and invent new fashions.

In all my professional life I have felt that in the plethora of choices only self-discipline would save an architect. How is it achieved? I have never had any doubt that the understanding of physical laws plus sympathy for people's needs and desires would give us the discipline needed to make architecture a consistent and convincing art. But "art" it must be, a striving of the spirit to express itself. Obviously, within such discipline there is the infinite variety of life itself. Within it, the artist-architect can find a whole range of expressions: the purposeful arrangement of human functions, from which beauty may emerge shining with the brightness of logic; the thoughtful and reassuring making of space, which shields man from infinity; the magnificent discoveries of the play of light and its delight for the human eye; the recognition of the human heart as the basis of wisdom.

Emerging social orders have tended to make architecture the servant of the masses, providing for them housing, shopping and recreation centers, schools, parks, and so on. This is a legitimate role; but in this, as in all roles, architecture must be yearning to express new symbols of our continuing humanity.

When we are made unhappy by the ugliness of our cities, our inner cry is for a return either to the serenity of the simple pastoral life of our forefathers or to the kind of city full of the rich and sensuous forms born in the great creative periods of the past. We seek "beauty," whatever we mean by that frayed and battle-scarred word. Unfortunately, the industrial revolution cannot be undone; still we persist in our search for a modern equivalent of beauty, and its mirage has led to all kinds of experiments, from sugary preciousness to brutalism, from revivals to surrealism to visionary architecture.

Some critics say that in many of these experiments we have failed because we have refused to learn with humility what nature has to teach us. They point out that beauty in nature is always an inherent quality of structural logic and appropriateness, yet never monotonous, in fact dazzling in its variety of forms. They claim that all we need to do is to observe it with intelligence and apply with discrimination the great technological knowledge placed at our disposal by science. This point of view is not shared by a vocal and most talented group of aesthetically minded designers who see architecture mainly as pure spirit, free from any rule, natural or structural. They care little for function or technology or social service. Architecture to them is mainly sculpture, a means of giving pure expression to abstract human ideals —in truth, the only humanistic exercise worthy of the name, an expression which seeks not human comfort or shallow beauty but affords the beholder the most profound experience and makes him proud of his power to participate in the search of abstract and harmonious order, a power similar to God's power. The attainment of such awareness, they say, is the true measure of man's progress as a civilized member of the race, and it is worth sacrificing convenience, comfort, and money. They dismiss other approaches as unworthy to be ranked with art and think of them as nothing more than mirrors of our decadent concern for material ends. They believe that our visual world is not determined by "forces" of practical nature but by the unique contributions of true artists.

Some time ago I had an interesting conversation on this point with Philip Johnson, who stated with his usual emphasis that

purpose is not necessary to make a building beautiful. Naturally we have to have some laboratories that work. In the Middle Ages it would not have been anything, but Wright had to rationalize or the Johnson Wax Company wouldn't have allowed him to build the Tower. It was the terrific problem of a man who wants a beautiful building but the only thing he has to build is a laboratory. Wright puts it into a tower. It doesn't work; it doesn't have to work. Wright had that shape conceived long before he knew what was going into it. I claim that is where architecture starts.

To my objections that just that was done in our worst periods of Greek or Gothic banks and libraries, he rejoined:

I would reverse everything you have said about the process of art. There is no search; there is no research. There is a discovery of form either here or in the air. Where form comes from I don't know, but it has nothing at all to do with the functional or sociological aspects of our architecture. It does not come from paintings. We will fit it to our sociological buildings, as Saarinen did to his buildings at M.I.T.; and sooner or later we will fit it so it can be used.

From such beliefs earnestly held, the pessimist will see only chaos emerging, but the optimist may believe that this pluralistic aspect of the art of architecture bespeaks the enormous potential of the human mind to attack our modern problems in a variety of ways, to seize all opportunities and challenges, to advance on many fronts with many tools and with open and free minds.

Unfortunately, a civilization is not constructed solely out of abstract ideas. Abstract ideas should rather serve to interpret the world of facts and events so that we may find meaning and direction in the course of life. Buildings, along with many other experiments, have tended to be ephemeral as change—more and more rapid—becomes a law of life. They partake of the obsolescence of things. The forming of an environment does not wait either on perfection or on well-thought-out programs and even less on the very few works by the great geniuses. Although every day it becomes more apparent that design and orderly thinking are needed in the creation of large suburban housing projects or in urban renewal or in the organization of factories and large commercial complexes, the time for mature thought or for grand strategy is lacking. So between change and improvisation, the meaning of architecture becomes diluted and equivocal; yet I never fail to sense the urgency of our present-day goals or the yearning which is voiced in many parts for fulfilment.

Then how will our environment be shaped? What must the standards be? What tools must be wrought? What social philosophies, what political means, must be invoked? And who are the all-wise men who can be trusted to lead? Are they to be architects, engineers, or imaginative artists? No one has the single answer. A pluralistic society lives and grows on confusion and conflict, and this idea must be accepted if we are to become useful and do our best in our own field.

In all creative arts, there are many levels by which works—from the carefully conceived and painstakingly detailed artifact to the great formal artistic conceptions by the great innovators—may be judged. Each work must be measured by standards appropriate to its level. Each feeds the spirit of man in its own way. Each is necessary in the complex balance of community living, a balance which in substance forms the culture of our society. For greatness, one may have to wait for geniuses to appear in great numbers, as in the best periods of the Renaissance, and have them place their powerful stamp on the ideas of a generation. But this sounds somewhat utopian, and there is much work which must be done now and cannot wait. Under present conditions, it is not easy for even a gifted architect to produce great works. Perhaps he will have to wait until our society is able to formulate great goals. A materialistic heaven of abundance, which is sought by all political systems, cannot give us more than a pattern of life. Only the passion aroused by deep beliefs in human destiny can arouse us to greatness. But although it is true that our passions now are soon spent on the surface of things, it would not be fair to say that the spirit is not yearning to emerge. We hear continually about the loss of our humanistic ideals, and we blame the machine or our politics, when in fact the means to express our humanity are created every day and everywhere. Even hideous wars are sparked by high emotions and ideals, such as freedom, equality, and justice, which fill the masses with enthusiasm, even if they do not always understand the hidden motives of their leaders. If we look deeply into our so-called materialistic community, we see that it will respond to any and all challenges of the spirit. Dormant or alive, there is in all of us a desire for higher, more satisfying, and more enduring goals—even if we do not know which are the important ones. Our artists consciously or unconsciously are groping for symbols. But symbols cannot be contrived. They are born out of the deep passions of people who are willing and capable of penetrating into the essence of things, who have vision to find its ultimate meaning and have the power to give it expression. In the meanwhile, it would be sad indeed if we could not make ourselves believe that slowly and tentatively we shall be able to establish visual order from chaos with full respect for the richness and variety of human life and that even the much-criticized American way will ultimately yield the essence of a good life and new aspects of beauty—the great ideal that is never possessed, yet is powerful enough to move every human being to its search.

Architects today must move between cosmic creativeness and mere virtuosity, between the grasping of new meanings and the refashioning of old ones, often succumbing to the superficialities of salesmanship, yet trying to find that uneasy balance between substance and expression where intellect does not surrender to emotion but rejoices in its presence. We must come to the conclusion that architecture, unlike other arts, is not an escape from but an acceptance of the human condition, from its many frailties to the technical advances of its scientists and engineers. It may rise to great art in a great society as it achieves unity, order, and form by appropriate technical means and as it meets its purposes with conviction. It appears to me that the great architect strives for comprehension rather than for originality for its own sake and that a thorough study of a problem, made in the freedom that knowledge provides, is always the greatest source of originality. It is the discipline of the intellect and the respect for the means at hand, therefore, that keep the architect from straying too far into the shallow waters of mere fashion.

It is interesting to note at this point that the idea of "art" as something separate from craftsmanship is comparatively new. In the Middle Ages, artisans, not "artists," built cathedrals which seem to us now the very peak of artistic expression. It was during the Renaissance that the artisan became the self-conscious, undisciplined, often arrogant "artist." Society used him for his ability to invent and above all to please but lost conviction in and authority over him as he became estranged from the stern demands of engineering and a practical-minded industrial society.

It is extremely important to have uncompromising artists in our midst; they are the very yeast of society. But the great mass of our buildings, the architecture of our cities, the whole background of our intense lives, are neither conceived nor built by artists but by engineers and technicians doing their limited best. The average architect has far too little to do with this work, unless he is willing to play an ambiguous role somewhere between engineer, technician, salesman, and fashion-seeker. If modern architecture is to express the symbols of our contemporary life, it must commit itself to the whole range of building activity, not to an insignificant sector of it. Human activity in the twentieth century is of infinite richness and variety. The search for truthful expression is enormously complex, and the conditions imposed by reality are so strict that they seldom allow the thoughtful choice between the significant and the trivial, the enduring and the transitory. In the final analysis, the environment of man is the consequence of what he believes to be important—the reflection of his own inner drive toward greater awareness and his concern for all human values.

The planning of cities requires a knowledge and wisdom not easily found in a single person, since the planner must be acquainted with political processes, economics, and social sciences, as well as possess the intuitive feeling of an artist sharpened by a lively interest in human beings. But human beings, both as individuals and in groups, are unpredictable in their behavior and desires. Frequently, certain urban features which may appear irrational to the planner may be more significant to the inhabitants than abstract, formal or rational relationships. This can be observed in certain nuclei of social life in so-called slums, which contain the very roots of community life even though the proper plumbing or parking may be lacking and the crowding may be great.

To speak of architecture as an art of our time, therefore, one must think of the human condition in our time—that people, like ants, spend their working day in a conformity of pursuits in the anonymity of the great cities. The ideas of usefulness and economy prevalent in our business world have so conditioned our actions that even beauty and grace, when allowed to exist, are discreetly asked to show a return on the investment—and what is strange and encouraging is that they are beginning to do so.

It has been said that art is a habit of the practical intellect. Its activity consists in impressing an idea upon matter; it resides in the mind; and its beauty has three requisites—integrity, proportion, and clarity. These requisites, then, could be the substance of our quest. As we try to understand our world, we may find that each new material demands its own technique, that each new technique develops its own language, and that in every language the human spirit may find poetic expression.

Poetry, however, needs the clear voices of people who know how to use language well and convincingly; and of these, there are only a few. So many voices arise to create confusion; and the advance of technical knowledge adds to the difficulty of bringing proportion or clarity to the modern scene. Unity or integrity is hard to achieve with present-day man's spiritual fragmentation. Architecture used to be essentially an aristocratic art for the prince and the church; it served the people only as a background for their activities. But now it has been placed at their everyday service. We find that this notion of service for the masses is a most difficult one to fit to the original idea of architecture as pure form. We have been at it for a hundred and fifty years, from the time of Jefferson and the simpler Georgian forms, but we haven't gotten very far yet. Perhaps there are too many people, and the means to cope with them, architecturally, politically, or spiritually, have escaped us.

The unbelievable extent to which the boundaries of knowledge are being expanded and the rapidity with which technology is keeping pace and changing the aspect of our civilization will cause greater change in our environment and in our way of life than anyone is able to imagine. The efforts to conquer stellar space and make man independent of the earth for long periods could conceivably revolutionize our urban systems, allowing people to live anywhere without water-supply or sewage-disposal systems or heating or cooling by fuel. Solar heat, low-power atomic reactors, or wind power, used in combination with compact compressors, could afford independent sources of energy; water from rain collected and used over and over could serve all the needs of a family; waste could be sterilized, compressed, and burned or disposed of in bulk. Greatly increased means of communication between individuals may affect our environment even more deeply than the expansion of knowledge, even if the essential nature of man, so emotionally tied to atavistic instincts, cannot be forced into artificial environments.

There are certain climates in the beliefs and habits of a society which allow the seeds of its creative minds to germinate into a great flowering of culture and in great works—fifth-century B.C. Athens, the Middle Ages in France, and the Italian Renaissance are the most conspicuous epochs that come to mind, where the power of the man and the power of the moment coincided. May we be allowed to dream that our society with all its shortcomings may be nourishing the seeds of new values through a continuous transformation and adaptation. The climate may again be favorable for the flowering of a great and humane civilization. There are some signs of our concern for a wide range of human expressions.

Thus far and on the whole, within their obvious limitations, architects have been men of vision. The leadership of the best of them has been in the humanistic field; they have proven by their works that they understood human goals and the fundamental need of mankind for artistic expression. Architecture, poetry, painting, and music have until recently offered the main channels for expression of the human spirit. The search for knowledge began early, too, and its recent orderly development has made it another large outlet for human aspiration. Each may in its own way be a search for truth; but none contains the whole truth. This final note is not one of pessimism but rather of admiration and hope for the human race.

Charles M. Goodman, FAIA, practicing architecture in Washington, D.C., is best known for advancing the design of American housing.

Mr. Goodman has worked with a variety of building types as an innovator and pioneer of modern architecture. His designs for federal buildings from 1934 to 1939 initiated the trend away from the Greco-Roman tradition toward contemporary solutions. During the Second World War he designed a series of airports and air terminals around the world, including the international air terminal at Washington National Airport. His early private residences were significant forerunners of modern domestic architecture. He was an early advocate of the sensitive use of rough wooded land and of new approaches to land planning, such as cluster houses around cul-de-sacs with dedicated park land between.

Mr. Goodman's intense interest in the industrialization of housing and its upgrading resulted in his working as consulting architect to National Homes Corporation for a number of years. His designs for the entire line evidenced his deep concern for diversity in houses even though their parts were standardized. He has extensively explored the use of old materials in new ways and the development of new materials. His research in aluminum led to the "Alcoa House of 1957" and the all-aluminum house of 1958. River Park, his urban renewal project in southwest Washington, D.C., for the Reynolds Metals Company, is a striking example of the special qualities of aluminum used in fresh ways.

Mr. Goodman's concern that the urban residential community have vitality at all hours of the day and night is presented in his recently published book, *Life for Dead Spaces*, coauthored with Wolf von Eckhardt and sponsored by the Lavanburg Foundation.

It is for his design of dwellings that Rice University especially honors Charles M. Goodman.

Charles M. Goodman / Architecture and Society

The simplicity and compelling nature of the force of a profession, with its emotional overtones that transcend the logic of modern society, can be expressed simply in the statement that the professional man must serve the life of his time by involving himself unremittingly in the rhythm of its flow with the hope that its course may be affected. I agree this is a heroic statement. I agree the vision of Don Quixote lurks uncomfortably near. And I agree this is not supposed to be the way to earn a living and get rich and famous in this society. But I am not convinced of any more realistic way to serve, no matter how pragmatic this society may become.

It has been said that the privileged, through their wealth and power, have been the sole possessors and arbiters of the means by which richness is added to man's environment and his life in his search for learning, his acts of prayer, and the fulfilling of his physical needs. Today, in theory, there are no such privileged in the society of free men we have wrought. The principle that we all have equal opportunity is deeply embedded in our mores. But the awesome responsibility, for every free man, that accompanies this principle is not as easily understood or accepted. In this respect we are not truly free men. And I cannot say we have been too successful in shouldering this responsibility. In point of fact, we are in danger of becoming a new and more refined society, refined in the degree of predatoriness—a predatoriness not simple and clean like that in the ecology of animal life.

When prehistoric man first raised his eyes to the sky and wondered, he unleashed thoughts and desires beyond his need for food and shelter that have plagued him through every stage in history. Because he thinks, feels, and wonders, he seeks—endlessly—with a hope that wanes and is revived by each succeeding generation. And with each succeeding generation, his environment's increasing complexity makes his search more and more difficult as well as less and less satisfying. According to biologists, man's ultimate achievement is his freedom from domination by his instincts, which are subject to his will in how he chooses to use them. But though he no longer has compulsive instincts like his relative, the monkey, Pavlov has demonstrated that he can still be reduced to an automatically acting, instinctive individual by conditioning his reflexes. Today, the conditioning he is exposed to is appalling in its breadth, intensity, and subtlety; and in too many situations, his automatic reactions are frighteningly close to those of the monkey. Thus, his search for some kind of fulfilment seems to have digressed from his nobler aspirations into the materialism of the latter half of the twentieth century, which unhappily recalls other such periods in the life of former great cultures. In this realm of aspiration, man seems to have forgotten or simply is not interested in the fact that he is a part of an infinitely complex structure of human life which, as a group of individuals, creates and passes on to history its own unique form of culture. We would do well to examine the evolving culture of our century with more care if we are not to degenerate into a society resembling that in Aldous Huxley's *Brave New World*, where the senses are titillated to the point of ever diminishing returns and man's heroic stance against his natural enemy, the hostile universe, is undermined.

I believe the profession of which I am a member faces the hazard of greater and greater alienation from the people of this society if its search continues for bigness and for clients who want to be remembered by monuments. I do not believe we can practice our profession of architecture or discuss it in terms as simple and sterile as abstract form, light and shade, historical form, precedent, function, economics, and so on, with any validity in a time and in a society as complex as ours. Nor do I believe that the struggle by many in our profession to identify themselves with the future through a unique work can ever produce anything other than a curiosity to the future historian.

Architecture in any period is what it is because the society that it more often than not reflects is what it is. To try and imbue a society with heroic qualities it does not possess through monumental works in the grand manner seems merely to point up the elusiveness of man's dream of his superiority and the meagerness of his aspirations. The awe-inspiring cathedral of the Gothic epoch was an exemplar of the struggle to create the illusion of a heroic society by means of an architecture of monumental proportions, an architecture which attempted to transcend space and mass through the dissolution of walls into an intricate tracery of stone and glass, ribs, vaults, and buttresses reaching farther and farther out into space. While the common man remained miserably poor and unlettered, all this attention was lavished on nothing more than a physical symbol of an age's fear of the unknown. Today, in what is supposedly a more sophisticated order of society, we clear slums and build "Centers of Culture," with meager knowledge and little feeling for the meaning and content, displacing the poor who have nowhere to go but into other more crowded slums. Education is mistrusted and taste is relegated to one of the minor needs of man's psyche, if recognized as a need at all. One of history's lessons provided by architecture is that man's works are perishable, even as he is, and that the general culture of his social period remains to be discovered by future generations. Here—in historical perspective through the artifacts of its culture—is where a society's place in history is determined.

That is why I see our profession's potential in the contribution it can make to the molding of the social body as a whole. Our cause and our struggle are to elevate the standards of the entire social body, not because the people have shown they want it, not because they will ever know or recognize it, not because they will reward us for it, but simply because man himself is a noble idea and we must endeavor to maintain standards if there is to be any meaning to his life. For this reason I believe that architecture *is* an art . . . but an art for the many. I do not believe architecture is structural expressionism, with its accompanying blatant dogma. This is only for the few who have the wealth with which to indulge their desire for new kicks. I do *not* believe "a street is trying to become a building" or that the entrails of the so-called serving spaces are compelled to be exposed. Nature hasn't done so in man, the most supreme act of creation. I see no reason for less discipline and modesty in architecture. I believe "less is more," only when "less" enriches the environment without redundance while adequately serving man's needs. "Less" for its own sake and the acceptance of less than the adequate serving of man's needs can be dignified by no other term than exhibitionism, of which there is already far too much in the life of our times.

It is difficult for me to say these things. I am no shrinking violet when arguing the case for responsible architecture with an inherent vital beauty that moves men's hearts, but I cannot find words simple enough or forceful enough or convincing enough to express the depth of my feeling about meaning and purpose in the practice of architecture. There is first dedication—by which I mean the dedication to one's profession as a way of life. There is understanding of and continuing concern for what past civilizations have learned and passed on to us. There is the stature necessary to recognize and preserve the best of what has been passed on to us as we seek our own way.

And there is restraint—of which there seems to be a limited supply in the practice of architecture today. One of the prerogatives which this free society seems to cherish is its right to disfigure its environment without restraint. But it ill becomes an honored and ancient profession to aid and abet this ugly trait by exercising so little restraint itself in what it creates and places on the land and explains away with wordy and esoteric apologias that are written after the fact.

The more one searches, hears, and sees, the more skeptical one becomes about the written and spoken words on architecture, the more one is inclined to do away with talk out of sheer embarrassment for the sterile nature of the architectural dialogue going on while the physical world in which we must live is such a shambles. Diana Rowntree has described this situation in the *Manchester Guardian* of December 27, 1962: "New words are added to all languages day by day, but I think American architects have carried the process of personal invention much too far, to the point where they are in effect using private languages." We are busily engaged in explaining design to ourselves in abstruse terms—which those who constitute our pragmatic society neither understand nor are much interested in—while their life flows turbulently on around us with little if any awareness that we exist. In short, there is no intelligible dialogue between the profession and society because we have made no effort to stimulate awareness of the need for our profession in terms that do not require an aesthetic interpreter. Why? Why must it be so? Why is a profession as honorable and ancient as that of architecture—the Art of Building, if you will—so utterly, completely, and hopelessly self-conscious? Why does it continue to mouth noble and ineffectual platitudes, meaningless to the man in the street? What is the terror which grips our profession making it scramble for favored position, building commissions, novelty, and glory at almost any price, to the point where the historic mission of the architect is lost or all but forgotten? Where is the social conscience that is aware that the serious corporate investor—the architectural patron of our time, who is primarily concerned with handling money, putting it to work, and realizing a return—retains the architect in the belief that, if benefits to the community are to accompany the return on the corporation's investment, it is within the architect's competence and it is his obligation to see that they are provided? Is not the familiar wail of our profession that benefits cost money and that the client is not willing to cough up such money unbecoming to the stature and creativity we profess? What has happened to the dignity of the professional man in modern life? Is terror so all-consuming that courage of ideals is now considered quaint? Where is the calm, judicious, creative professional mind, truly concerned with the needs, wants, and weaknesses of his fellow man and determined to provide him with beauty as well, at a price he can afford? Where is the humility of the truly creative mind which searches for the truth—endlessly? And where *is* the truth in architecture today in the latter half of the twentieth century?

It takes a terrible struggle within one's self not to conclude that this profession is even more dishonest in its pretensions than the society that harbors it. And it takes Herculean faith not to conclude that man, the noble idea, may be all tinsel and the idea discredited. But I cannot believe that, and I never will. For to cease to reach for nobility in man is to cease to live a fruitful life, fruitful in the degree that it is dedicated to the expansion and perpetuation of a human culture worthy of being recorded in history, which is the only meaningful aim I can see in man's life on this earth.

Marshall Shaffer

Marshall Shaffer worked with the federal government in developing better hospitals across the nation.

Mr. Shaffer began his professional life as a civil engineer but later turned to architecture. He was constantly aware of the social responsibility of architecture; and when he taught design at Pratt Institute, it was always against a background of economics and sociology.

In 1941, he joined the U.S. Public Health Service as a planning consultant—the first architect ever to serve with this agency. With the passage of the Hill-Burton act for the construction of hospitals in 1946, he began to compile a complete set of standards for hospital design; he drew upon the resources of every related field and finally organized his ideas and information into a book, *Elements of Hospital Planning*, a basic guide for hospital architects. The work of Shaffer's staff was directed largely toward research and education, for he saw the federal government not as an architectural board but rather as a source of information and stimulation for individual architects. The program that he set up included local architects as designers—most of whom had never before designed a hospital—and his staff as resource material and advisors. Through this plan, modern, efficient hospitals have been constructed in all parts of the United States, and innumerable architects have been educated in the special problems and philosophies that influence hospital design. In 1951 the American Institute of Architects presented its coveted Kemper Award to Mr. Shaffer.

Marshall Shaffer has been honored posthumously by Rice University for his contribution to the design of hospitals.

Plates

John Lyon Reid, Aragon High School,
San Mateo, California (*Roger Sturtevant*)

John Lyon Reid, Hillsdale High School,
San Mateo, California (*Roger Sturtevant*)

John Lyon Reid, Health Sciences Instruction and
Research Laboratory, University of California Medical Center,
San Francisco, California (*Dwain Faubion*)

O'Neil Ford, Texas Instruments,
Dallas, Texas (*N. Bleecker Green*)

O'Neil Ford, Interior of Texas Instruments,
Dallas, Texas (*N. Bleecker Green*)

O'Neil Ford, Planetarium and Observatory,
St. Mark's School of Texas, Dallas, Texas (*John Rogers*)

Victor Gruen, Plan for Fort Worth, Texas
(*Gordon Sommers*)

Victor Gruen, Southdale Shopping Center,
Minneapolis, Minnesota (*Warren Reynolds—Infinity, Inc.*)

Victor Gruen, "The Rocks,"
Sidney, Australia (*Gordon Sommers*)

I. M. Pei, The Luce Chapel, Tunghai University,
Taichung, Taiwan (*Chi-kwan Chen*)

I. M. Pei, Denver Hilton Hotel,
Denver, Colorado (*Guy Burgess*)

I. M. Pei, Washington Square East,
Philadelphia, Pennsylvania (*George Cserna*)

Vernon DeMars

Vernon DeMars, Student Center, University of California,
Berkeley, California (*Morley Baer*)

Vernon DeMars, Urban Renewal Project, "The Golden Gateway,"
San Francisco, California (*Gerald Ratto*)

Vernon DeMars, Urban Renewal Proposal,
Santa Monica, California (*Barry Evans*)

Pietro Belluschi, Portsmouth Priory,
Portsmouth, Rhode Island (*Joseph W. Molitor*)

Pietro Belluschi

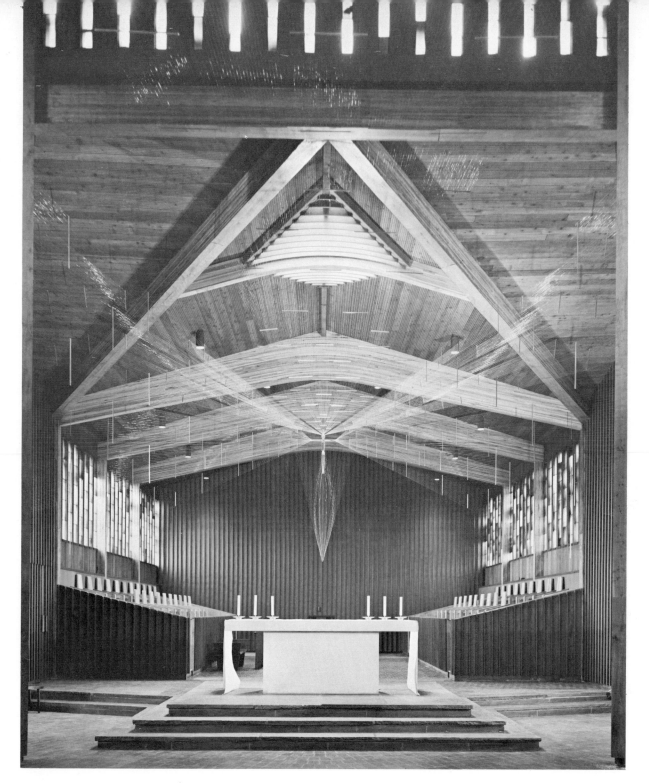

Pietro Belluschi, Interior of Portsmouth Priory,
Portsmouth, Rhode Island (*Joseph W. Molitor*)

Pietro Belluschi

Pietro Belluschi, Library of Bennington College,
Bennington, Vermont (*Ezra Stoller*)

Pietro Belluschi

Charles M. Goodman, Residence for Mr. and Mrs. Wayne Parrish,
Washington, D.C. (*Davis Studio*)

Charles M. Goodman, River Park S.W.,
Washington, D.C. (*Robert C. Lautman*)

Charles M. Goodman, River Park S.W.,
Washington, D.C. (*Robert C. Lautman*)